D0065248

NORTH SARASOTA
PUBLIC LIBRARY
2801 NEWTOWN BLVD.
SARASOTA, FL 34234

African American Cultural Theory and Heritage

Series Editor: William C. Banfield

In the Heart of the Beat

The Poetry of Rap

African American Cultural Theory and Heritage

NORTH SARASOTA
PUBLIC LIBRARY
2801 NEWTOWN BLVD.
SARASOTA, FL 34234

Alexs Pate

THE SCARECROW PRESS, INC.
Lanham, Maryland • Toronto • Plymouth, UK
2010

3 1969 01700 1016

SCARECROW PRESS, INC.

Published in the United States of America
by Scarecrow Press, Inc.
A wholly owned subsidary of
The Rowman & Littlefield Publishing Group, Inc.
4501 Forbes Boulevard, Suite 200, Lanham, Maryland 20706
www.scarecrowpress.com

Estover Road
Plymouth PL6 7PY
United Kingdom

Copyright © 2010 by Alexs Pate

All rights reserved. No part of this publication may be reproduced,
stored in a retrieval system, or transmitted in any form or by any
means, electronic, mechanical, photocopying, recording, or otherwise,
without the prior permission of the publisher.

British Library Cataloguing in Publication Information Available

Library of Congress Cataloging-in-Publication Data

Pate, Alexs D.
 In the heart of the beat : the poetry of rap / Alexs D. Pate.
    p. cm. — (African American cultural theory and heritage)
 Includes bibliographical references and index.
 ISBN 978-0-8108-6008-7 (cloth : alk. paper)
  1. Rap (Music)—Texts. 2. Rap (Music)—History and criticism. 3. American poetry—
African American authors—History and criticism. I. Title. ML3531.P38 2009
 782.421649—dc22
                            2008049295

∞ ™ The paper used in this publication meets the minimum requirements of American
National Standard for Information Sciences—Permanence of Paper for Printed Library
Materials, ANSI/NISO Z39.48-1992.

For the pioneers whose words carried their own beats and pumped new life into contemporary poetic expression.

The form that's burned into my soul is some twisted awful thing that crept in from a dream, a goddamn nightmare, an' won't stay still unless I feed it. An' it lives on words. Not beautiful words. God Almighty no.

—*Cane* by Jean Toomer

Contents

Praise and Shouts

This book truly is a labor of many people. First I'd like to thank the series editor, William "Bill" Banfield, for the many hours of "engagement" as I worked through the issues of this book. I used Bill as a target on occasion as I tried to hone my arguments. He fought back with his usual tenacity and vivacity. This made the process intense and fun for me especially since it was always in the presence of partners and good food. It might have been a bit boring for them perhaps, but essential for me. This book is definitely richer for the experience. Thanks also to Ed Kurdyla, publisher of Scarecrow, for his belief in this book and to Corinne Burton, who carefully guided it through the system.

Because of the volume and velocity of this art form, and because much of the best of rap is hidden or hard to locate, I continue to depend on my students to help keep me current. So, this book truly comes from and through the labor of many people. It has my voice at its center, but each and every student who has studied with me or engaged me in debate fuels it. Many students and colleagues helped with this project. Of special note is the contribution of Paul Boyer, who from the outset worked very closely with me on this effort, providing encouragement and research support. His contribution was both substantive and inspirational. As an assistant in my classroom for four years, Paul brought an intellectual curiosity and knowledge of rap that offered my students an exponentially deeper inquiry in the poetry of rap.

The painstaking early work of compiling the anthology of rap/poems and the refinement of the ideas that run through this effort come as the result of long discussions between Paul and me. Paul and those many students pushed me with their questions, disagreements, challenges, and brilliant inquiry. That crucible of discourse has, in many ways, defined the form of what follows.

As this book took shape, Ian Mullins took over for Paul and helped me hone the class into a laboratory for the necessary work that was required to make the class and this book symbiotic in nature. Our discussions before, during, and after class helped me codify the small incremental movement of my own ideas about rap/poetry.

As I worked through the implications of some of the ideas expressed in this book, many students played a major role. They brought forth obscure and significant rap/poems. They transcribed and tested the efficacy of my ideas about rap/poetics on the popular songs of the day. Of these students, none has been more helpful or covered more ground than Hodges Glenn. Even though he joined my team late, his research support and thinking about the rap music that informs his life certainly helped me apply and validate the ideas that are presented in this book. His relentless energy for understanding the complexity of rap/poetry was energizing. Alicia Steele brought a sharp and sensitive eye to the process of codifying and "intellectualizing" the lives and aspirations of real people.

When I published my first novel, *Losing Absalom*, I thanked the world. Now, with this work, I feel the same way. The shouts are real and heartfelt, expansive and effusive. Still, I know I will omit someone. I ask for your forgiveness if I missed you.

Thanks to Gyanni Pate, Alexs Jr., David Mura, Susan Sencer, Ralph Remington, Damu McCoy, J. Otis Powell!, Sunmee Chomet, William Banfield, Krystal Banfield, John Wright, Serena Wright, Tom Nelson, Keith Mayes, Quincy Troupe, E. Ethelbert Miller, Manisha Nordine, Perry Silverman, Doris Yock, Walter Jacobs, Rose Brewer, Kimlar Satterthwaite, Tai Coleman, Ezra Hyland, May Fu, Njeri Githrie, Trica Keaton, Caron Umbarger, Paul Umbarger, Napoleon Andrews, Archie Givens, Carol Meshbesher, Paul Boyer, Ian Mullins, Rachel Raimist, Hodges "Eddie" Glenn, Alicia Steele, Margaret Majewski, Nneka Onyilofor, Emily Corrigan, Tomo and Nikko Mura, Jeb Middlebrook, Mandy Podransky, Michael Hastert, Leslie DuCloux, Toki Wright, Sheryl Wilson, Me-K Ahn, Phillippe Gills, Anna Kuharjec, Blake Iverson, Sean McPherson, Ali Elabbady, Amber Cleveland, Thomas Horgen, Carson Friend, Caleb Truax, Benjamin Jamison, Michelle Kwan, Jessi Lynch, Benjamin Lenyard, Marcus Lewis, Quentin White, Shirani Jayasuriya, Sage Francis, I Self Devine, Rodrigo Sanchez, Ben Jamison, Abdel Shakur, Devin Swanson, Amber Swanson, Renee Baron, e.g. bailey, Sha Cage, Arletta Little, Brandon, Carolyn Holbrook Montgomery, Jeff Hom, Alexander Roberts, Mike Riehle, Jason Shogren, Jerry Vallery, Dexter Davis, Barrett Patin, Jessica Phillips, Mankwe Ndosi, Cheryl Floyd-Miller, All Day, Cynthia Gehrig, and the Jerome Foundation.

To SooJin, my wife, I can only say, yet again, how lucky I am. Besides the fact that you read this book and gave me editing suggestions more times than you probably wanted to, it is in this world with you and our daughter Sxela that I am able to do this work.

Sections of this book, in various versions, have appeared in *Colors* magazine, the *Washington Post*, and *USA Today Magazine*.

Preface and DISclaimas

The world of hip hop and rap is in constant motion; consequently, impressions and thoughts about its meaning, power, and dimension are perpetually challenged. There have been times when I was sure that the white-hot impact of hip hop on American culture had reached its zenith and was on the verge of dissipating into the same pit as the shingaling or the Watusi (two dances that entranced black bodies in the 1960s). Perhaps, I reasoned, if it did disappear from our contemporary consciousness, I would be spared the mysterious compulsion to love it, and consequently, because I love it so much, I would be spared from having to write and talk about it. But, alas, as I write this, the reverberations of rap and hip hop continue to grow.

Somewhere someone is bemoaning the negative impact of rap music on American and/or African American culture. Somewhere someone has targeted yet another example of insipid, violent, or sexually deviant ideas being perpetrated by yet another irresponsible rapper. It wasn't that long ago that African American women were up in arms at the latest affront to their sensibilities and public image when the video manifestation of Nelly's "Tip Drill" was released. Then there was the sudden eruption of consciousness and reprimand from Bill Cosby as he ventured forth with his excoriating attack on the social, moral, and intellectual condition of black folks in America. There he stood, the icon supreme of black middle-class values and aspirations of the 1980s and 1990s, fully bearing the cloak of his Huxtable identity to admonish folks (black folks) to take greater responsibility for their failures of mobility and viability in contemporary American society. Embedded in Cosby's message, as it is in many missives from the middle class, was the clear accusation that contemporary African American culture was infested with the negative energy of hip hop.

During the historic presidential campaign of 2008, candidate Barack Obama, an African American, was challenged by his critics to explain his appreciation of the "talent" of rapper Ludacris. At the same time, Nas released a rap/poem in which he expressed a desire that the newly elected Obama paint the White House black.

Let us simply accept that there is and always will be some form of beef and controversy swirling around rap and hip hop. And while these controversies and arguments are slightly beyond my interests, they in fact validate my curiosity about rap. Thinking about this takes me back to the day I decided to explore, more thoroughly, the details of this art form. It was the day I walked the halls of a high school in Bemidji, Minnesota, of all places. I was there as a visiting writer-in-residence, and as I walked out of my classroom and headed down the hall, a skinny white kid came sauntering my way. He had earphones on which were connected to a Sony Walkman. And while I couldn't hear what he was listening to, I could hear him clearly:

> You know I'm proud to be black y'all
> and that's a fact y'all
> And if you try to take what's mine
> I take it back y'all—it's like that

He was rapping right along with Run DMC ("Proud to Be Black"). Did I mention that he was white? It stunned me. I was already consumed by rap. It was all I listened to. But *I* listened to it because I was stranded in Minnesota, far away from the heart of darkness, North Philadelphia, where I had grown up. I could pull up some Schoolly D, or later the Roots, and immediately feel the Philly vibe. Rap provided me with a sense of home, a way of knowing what was going on with the people I'd left behind. And I loved words, the poetry of rap music. I used this new sound as one way to stay immersed in black culture, even as I tried to survive in the cold, white Midwest. But what was this kid getting out of it?[1]

That question and scores more lured me deeper into contemplating the significance of rap music in my life. Still, it's one thing to think about rap and quite another to feel competent enough to write about it.

I am, to be clear, quite simply a writer, a poet, and a teacher. I've been listening to rap for nearly its entire life span—a full thirty years or more. And although I am a resident in the center slice of the Midwest, far from the roiling streets that gave birth to hip hop and rap, it has become as natural to my spirit as Miles Davis, Pharoah Sanders, Jimi Hendrix, or Smokey Robinson and the Miracles. I am as anxious and excited as people much younger than me when I know the Roots or Little Brother are about to drop a new joint.

The hip hop beat is everywhere. You can find it pulsating on the radio or bouncing off the walls of nightclubs. It has become the background beat of Cadillac commercials and breakfast cereals. You might even call it the "theme beat" of our times.

Unfortunately, in my opinion, many people often confuse the "beat" of hip hop with rap. I'm reminded of a television commercial that was simply a tightly edited series of stellar basketball dribblers, doing what they did best on a sound-enhanced floor. The resonant percussive sounds they made as they dribbled the basketball were meant to, and did in fact, mimic the hip hop beat.

We watched and listened as those adept basketball players became the hip hop beat. Not one word was spoken. One dribbler after another produced his or her contribution to the collective beat. The first time I saw it, it was a marvel. But after watching that commercial over and over, I realized it left a rather negative residue. It did indeed validate hip hop culture, demonstrating quite effectively the infectiousness and unpredictability of hip hop on the one hand. But it was also quite clear that, at the same time, it was exploiting it, sucking the life out of this vibrant, street-based cultural reality.

This is what American popular media do, especially with music. They replicate, repeat, and wear out anything that has demonstrated a capacity to be popular, particularly if that thing—in this case rap music—can be used to sell other things, namely cars, cereal, and so forth. This happens until people are tired of hearing it and decide there must be something else to watch or listen to or talk about. In time that beat or sound or style is no longer popular and is relegated to the storage bin of oldies shows and revivals. With most of the superficial elements of popular culture, this process serves society quite nicely.

But the poetic aspirations and accomplishments in rap should not run the risk of being discarded when America tires of the beat. More to the point, the words—in the case of rap—are more important than the music. Rap/poetry (formally defined later) is an important link in the evolution of African American literature, and just as significant, an accurate and compelling window into black consciousness. Exhilarating and troubling at the same time, rap/poetry also presents a unique African American commentary on contemporary economics, ethics, morality, politics, foreign policy, sexuality, and tolerance among a too-long-to-list range of topics. It is a cultural expression that has revealed no limitations in its breadth of focus.

What makes this cultural expression particularly important is that many rappers use complex techniques of poetic structure in their work. There is immense skill involved in creating rap/poetry that is both meaningful and structurally advanced. These poets are not often given credit in the world of poetry and art for what they do.

Perhaps even more significant is that rap/poetry has become the first exported *literary* form that has emanated from African American culture. People are using this art form in the favelas of Rio, in the tight allies of the Palestine territories, in urban Havana. There are rap/poets at work in Russia and China. Throughout Europe and Asia, the poetry of rap resonates.

One can also witness the explosion of rap/poetic expression on the African continent, which is interesting for many reasons, the most profound being that African American expression (all African American expression) began in Africa. In contemporary Ghana, South Africa, Nigeria, and many other African countries, the American style of rap has emerged as one of the fundamental forms of contemporary expression. Over time, in each country where rap/poetry has become a part of the cultural landscape, the native language has been converted in the same way that American English was converted and then re-imagined in a rap/poetic way.

Although serious exploration of hip hop culture and rap music are appearing with more frequency on college campuses and in high school classrooms, most of the ensuing discussion is often focused on the sound of it and its cultural implications. Many teachers and their students are exploring such questions as: What is the history of this cultural phenomenon? How is hip hop changing American society? What does hip hop and rap say about the sociology of urban life? These and other questions are important, but they hardly address issues of quality in the expression itself.

Many books about hip hop and rap focus on social, political, economic, technological, and community-oriented issues, using the words of the rap/poems as evidence of some condition or circumstance. Other books provide historical documentation of its evolution and its impact. But little serious work exists that embraces rap as a poetic reality.[2] This is the primary purpose of this book. It "reads" rap/poetry in such a way that its inherent poetic qualities are explored.

This way of reading may or may not correspond to any standing literary critical theory, but it does identify a way of reading rap/poetry that encourages the reader to step beyond the dominance of the beat and to see rap/poetry's many dimensions. It is an approach to rap/poetry that allows the reader to make judgments about its construction, its durability, and even its meaning. And, it is an approach that is based on the components within rap/poetry. I have tried not to superimpose an external system of critical review, but rather I have tried to look at rap/poetry from the inside out (to the degree that I am able) to identify, define, and discuss its elements.

While this book does not attempt to interpret the impact of music on the development of rap/poetry, it is absolutely clear that without music as a viable mechanism for delivering the words to the listeners, rap might have well become what most people thought it was at its inception: a fad. But the presence of music and the centrality of music in the lives of African Americans offered the ideal petri dish for poetic experimentation. Indeed, the music of rap is largely a music of the past. The DJs, those who provide the beats, reach back most often to the same beats that moved their parents. They perfume the air with beats made popular by Sly Stone; Earth, Wind & Fire; George Clinton; James Brown; the Ohio Players; and so forth. It was the poets who discovered the power that those comfortable, looped, and sampled beats provided. The poets discovered that when the beat was just right, you could say almost anything.

It is true, of course, that the beat is the lure, the open arms of hip hop. For many, the beat seduces, recalls the strength of the past. The beat of rap is often the sonic, pulsating air of a particular street corner, the thumping bass moving the crowd at a club, or that intense moment of danger and threat that happens when folks wind up in the wrong place at the wrong time.

Rap also has a deeper connection to black cultural history, as it flows directly from its musical, performative, and literary antecedents. The black voice spoke out sharply in the fields as work songs, on the chain gangs as prison songs, and on urban corners with the "dozens." The black voice showed up on the radio with the rapping radio jockeys of the 1950s and 1960s. It was present in Muhammad Ali and a host of black male and female comedians like Pigmeat Markham, Richard Pryor, Moms Mabley, Dolemite, and Redd Foxx, and in the crazy uncle in everybody's family who knew everything about everybody and always found a way to demonstrate it with a long, funny story. It was in the pulpit and the sweet, natural, effortless rap of brothers and sisters showered in blue light at a Saturday-night house party. All of this and more are a part of the literary evolution of rap/poetry.

From those derivations rap has bloomed into a sturdy, morphing, dynamic poetic organism. It has withstood the transition of three generations of urban youth, all the time maintaining its allure with their white suburban counterparts.

But when the general public turns to discuss rap, it is almost never about the surprising skill and power of these poets. It is usually about a profane idea or action that is described in one of the poems. And predictably, from a literary standpoint, the typical offending pieces almost never merit the attention they receive. Neither 2 Live Crew's "Me So Horny," Ice T's "Kill Tha Police," or Nelly's "Tip Drill"—all igniting some degree of national concern—fare well in a literary analysis.

It is important that the truth of the words—the power, plaint, and artistry of the poems that ride the waves of refried R&B, funk, and jazz—not be lost to the cynical exploitation of popular media and the mistaken belief that what people *think they know* about rap condemns it as a negative contribution to popular culture.

I hope this attempt to articulate a sense about what rap is to me, and how I evaluate its quality, will be seen as a necessary addition to the conversation about rap. In the end, I suppose it was the fact that I had accumulated a lot of information over the ten years or so of teaching the course that forms the basis of this book, along with a sense of comfort I had with that experience, that beckoned me forth.

As I've noted, the shape of this book reflects a way of thinking. The earlier chapters focus primarily on the aspects of context that are necessary to understand the artistic realities of rap/poetry. Once a context has been established, the elements of a critical review of rap/poetry are presented, leading to a discussion of the relevance and quality of its literary significance.

There are many issues that confronted my intentions with this work. For example, how do you deal with a poem that has been written by more than one person? This is often true in rap/poetry. Rap/poets have traditionally shared the space and the page with each other. But multiple speakers in individual rap poems complicate the process of critique. Before rap/poetry, the art and craft of this demanding form was generally a solitary endeavor.

My approach to this is to privilege all speakers in a poem individually. That is, in a poem like "Respiration" by Blackstar, which includes poetry by three poets, Talib Kweli, Mos Def, and Common (formerly Common Sense), I might examine each poet's contribution separately to consider its effectiveness. Then my attention would flow to the whole. The final consideration might be how well these poets fuse their individual contributions to create the larger poem, allowing us the opportunity to evaluate it as a "whole" expression.

I was crestfallen when I learned that some rap artists use ghostwriters to produce the poems for them to perform. This marked another indication that the "business" of rap threatened the art of it. To the best of our knowledge, the poems in *In the Heart of the Beat: The Poetry of Rap* were all written by the persons registered for copyright. But in a way, the actual authorship of a given rap/poem is less significant when it is the quality of the poem that is in focus. The essential point of this book is that what most people consider "music" is, in fact, "poetry."

The sheer size of this body of poetry is prodigious, and I make no claims that this study has considered every published rap/poem. The created names and nicknames of the rappers might be cause for some to dismiss the work as not being worthy of serious literary consideration. At best, the world outside of hip hop can only wonder about someone who goes by the name of Ghostface Killah or J-Live or CL Smooth. Many of the performers are not as comfortable as Kanye West when it comes to using their given names. There is a book waiting to be written about the reasons and implications of rap/poets who take on alternate public personas. It is not, however, this book, so we have tried to withstand the ambient pressure to marginalize the poets we've examined.

But it must be said that despite our desire to recognize and celebrate the best rap/poems and their makers, our emphasis is most decidedly on the poem itself and not the poet. In this regard, we felt justified in using excerpts to make specific points in the narrative. (We hope that all poems discussed in the narrative can be subsequently published in their entirety as an anthology.) In addition, because this book is focused on the poetry, it is not about evaluating any particular rap/poet's entire body of work. In fact, it is important to be able to identify the gems, even if they are rare, by any particular rap/poet. For example, Too $hort's catalog of poems is notoriously focused on sex, street struggles, and various aspects of what some might call "thug life." But he also wrote a poem called "The Ghetto," which is a powerful discussion of inner-city life.

> Even though they put us down and call us animals
> We make real big banks and buy brand new clothes
> Drive fancy cars, make love to stars
> Never really saying just who we are
> We use alias names like TOO $HORT
> Sell you stuff you might kill for
> Young kids grow up and that's all they know
> Didn't teach him in school now he's slangin dope
> Only thing he knows is how to survive
> But will he kill another brother before he dies?
> In the ghetto, you keep one eye open
> All day long, just hoping and hoping
> You can pay your bills and not drink too much
> Then the problems of life you'll be throwing up
> Like me, but you don't see
> Ten years from now, where will you be?
> The ghetto
> The ghetto
> (Talking 'bout the ghetto)
> The ghetto
> The ghetto
> (Funk funky ghetto)

It is important to me that that poem, as an example of others, be liberated from a stereotyped gangsta rap/poet's repertoire. I'm not here to tell Too $hort what to write about. But, for me, "The Ghetto" is a classic that established his poetic skill.

So, this book provides no comprehensive review of Tupac Shakur, Notorious B.I.G., Apani B, or any rap/poet for that matter. Our goal is simply to suggest a way of reading rap that reveals the genius of many of the poems to collect some of the best in we hope a future anthology.

I do want to say that the history of rap/poetry is vast and expanding every day and consequently the desire to be comprehensive is a futile one. I would love to spend more time with the work of Big Daddy Kane, Ice T, Atmosphere, Sage Francis, Cypress Hill, The Beastie Boys, Mos Def, De La Soul, Mob Deep, Brother Ali, Outkast, Blue Scholars, Immortal Technique, or scores of other good rap/poets but the limitations of this endeavor prevent it.

There is also a need to address the diversity of readers that might be drawn to this book. On the one hand, *In the Heart of the Beat* is meant to convince its readers of the importance of rap/poetry. The presumption is that a great number of people, even people who listen regularly to rap music, don't listen carefully. They don't "read" rap in the way that I hope will be possible by the time this book is digested.

But I know that there is also a vibrant, literate, streetwise population of rap "readers" who care about what rap/poets say. They can quote popular and obscure rap/poetry effortlessly, understanding all of its meanings and implications. Much of what I write in this book they already know. They know it intuitively and don't really need me or anyone else to validate rap's literary significance.

There are, in fact, many people who love rap, who are committed to hip hop and are still dismayed at the amount of energy and language it requires to establish its literary significance. They would much rather have a conversation in which the artistic quality and effectiveness of rap as a literary expression were a given. And I wish, for my own selfish purposes, that I were writing to an entirely sympathetic readership. But my momma didn't raise no . . . ya know? I know who I'm talking to. Fa sho'.

Still, it is my hope that *In the Heart of the Beat* will contribute to the growing discussion of a rap aesthetic and specifically an organized way of "reading" the poetry that drives it.

NOTES

1. Bakari Kitwana was also intrigued by this question and attempts an answer in *Why White Kids Love Hip Hop: Wankstas, Wiggers, Wannabes, and the New Reality of Race in America* (Basic Civitas Books, 2005).

2. One notable exception is Imani Perry's *Prophets of the Hood: Politics and Poetics in Hip Hop* (Duke University Press, 2004), which engages its reader in a serious literary and cultural critique of the language and modes of poetic expression in rap.

Permissions

50 YEARS
Written by David J. Kelly of All Natural
Copyright © 1998 All Natural, Inc.
All Rights Reserved. Permission Granted.

THE 6TH SENSE (SOMETHING U FEEL)
Words and Music by Kejuan Muchita, Albert Johnson, Lonnie Rashid Lynn, Christopher Martin and Bilal Oliver
© 2000 EMI APRIL MUSIC INC., GIFTED PEARL MUSIC, UNIVERSAL MUSIC—MGB SONGS, JUVENILE HELL, UNIVERSAL MUSIC—CAREERS, P. NOID PUBLISHING, SONGS OF UNIVERSAL, INC., SENSELESS MUSIC, INC., WARNER-TAMERLANE PUBLISHING CORP. and JAZZMEN PUBLISHING
All Rights for GIFTED PEARL MUSIC Controlled and Administered by EMI APRIL MUSIC INC.
All Rights for JUVENILE HELL Administered by UNIVERSAL MUSIC—MGB SONGS
All Rights for P. NOID PUBLISHING Administered by UNIVERSAL MUSIC—CAREERS
All Rights for SENSELESS MUSIC, INC. Controlled and Administered by SONGS OF UNIVERSAL, INC.
All Rights for JAZZMEN PUBLISHING Administered by WARNER-TAMERLANE PUBLISHING CORP.
All Rights Reserved. International Copyright Secured. Used by Permission.
Contains a sample of "Allustrious" by Kejuan Muchita and Albert Johnson.

ALIVE ON ARRIVAL
Words and Music by O'SHEA JACKSON, MARK JORDAN, TEREN JONES, GEORGE CLINTON, JR., RONALD DUNBAR AND DONNIE RAY STERLING
Copyright © 1991 WB MUSIC CORP. (ASCAP), GANGSTA BOOGIE MUSIC (ASCAP), STREET KNOWLEDGE PRODUCTIONS (ASCAP) and BRIDGEPORT MUSIC, INC. (BMI)
All Rights on Behalf of Itself and GANGSTA BOOGIE MUSIC Administered by WB MUSIC CORP.
All Rights Reserved. Used By Permission of ALFRED PUBLISHING CO., INC.

THE ART OF STORYTELLIN' PART 1
Words and Music by David Sheats, Andre Benjamin and Antwan Patton
©1998 EMI APRIL MUSIC INC., DUNGEON RAT MUSIC, CHRYSALIS MUSIC and GNAT BOOTY MUSIC
All Rights for DUNGEON RAT MUSIC Controlled and Administered by EMI APRIL MUSIC INC.
All Rights for GNAT BOOTY MUSIC Controlled and Administered by CHRYSALIS MUSIC
All Rights Reserved. International Copyright Secured. Used by Permission.

BETWEEN ME, YOU, & LIBERATION
Words and Music by Ahmir Thompson, Lonnie Rashid Lynn, James Poyser, James Yancey, Pino Palladino and Thomas Callaway
Copyright © 2002 UNIVERSAL—POLYGRAM INTERNATIONAL PUBLISHING, INC., UNIVERSAL MUSIC CORP., SONGS OF UNIVERSAL, INC., UNIVERSAL MUSIC— CAREERS, E.P.H.C.Y. PUBLISHING, JAJAPO MUSIC, SENSELESS MUSIC, GRAND NEGAZ MUSIC, FLASH GORDON MUSIC, ONIP MUSIC and GOD GIVEN MUSIC
All Rights for E.P.H.C.Y. PUBLISHING Controlled and Administered by UNIVERSAL— POLYGRAM INTERNATIONAL PUBLISHING, INC.
All Rights for JAJAPO MUSIC Controlled and Administered by UNIVERSAL MUSIC CORP.
All Rights for SENSELESS MUSIC, INC. Controlled and Administered by SONGS OF UNIVERSAL, INC.
All Rights for GRAND NEGAZ MUSIC Controlled and Administered by UNIVERSAL MUSIC—CAREERS
All Rights for ONIP MUSIC Controlled and Administered by BUG MUSIC, INC.
All Rights Reserved. Used by Permission.

"BLACK ART"
© Amiri Baraka
Used with permission by the author.

BLOCK PARTY
Written by Jean Grae (T. Ibrahim)
Copyright © 2002 Liu Sing Publishing ASCAP
All Rights Reserved. Used by Permission.

THE BREAKS
Written by J. Moore, L. Smith, K. Blow, R. Ford, R. Simmons
Copyright © 1980 Neutral Gray Music
All Rights Reserved. Permission Granted.

BUST A MOVE
Words and Music by Marvin Young and Matt Dike
Copyright © 1989 Varry White Music, Inc., Young Man Moving, Inc. and Ex VW, Inc.
All Rights for Varry White Music, Inc. and Young Man Moving, Inc. Administered by Spirit Two Music, Inc. (ASCAP)
All Rights for Ex VW, Inc. Administered by Bug Music
International Copyright Secured. All Rights Reserved.

CAN'T TRUSS IT
Words and Music by Carlton Ridenhour, James Boxley III and Gary Rinaldo
Copyright © 1991 SONGS OF UNIVERSAL, INC., TERRORDOME MUSIC PUBLISHING LLC, BRING THE NOIZE, INC., SHOCKLEE MUSIC and SUBFUNK MUSIC
All Rights Reserved. Used by Permission.

DEAR MAMA
Words and Music by Tony Pizarro, Joseph Sample and Tupac Shakur
Copyright © 1995 UNIVERSAL MUSIC CORP., SONGS OF UNIVERSAL, INC., FOUR KNIGHTS MUSIC CO., WB MUSIC CORP. and THE UNDERGROUND CONNECTION
All Rights for THE UNDERGROUND CONNECTION Administered by WB MUSIC CORP.
All Rights Reserved. Used by Permission.
Contains elements from "Sadie" (Joseph Jefferson/Bruce Hawes/Charles Simmons), WARNER-TAMERLANE PUBLISHING CORP.

EBONICS
Words and Music by Rondell Turner and Lester Coleman
Copyright © 2000 SONGS OF UNIVERSAL, INC., NOTTING HILL MUSIC, INC. BROWZ MUSIC and LESTER COLEMAN
All Rights for NOTTING HILL MUSIC, INC. and BROWZ MUSIC Controlled and Administered by SONGS OF UNIVERSAL, INC.
All Rights Reserved. Used by Permission.

FOR WOMEN
Words and Music by Talib Kweli and Tony Cottrell
Copyright © 2000 Songs Of Windswept Pacific, DJ Hi Tek Music Publishing and Pen Skills Music
All Rights Administered by Songs Of Windswept Pacific
All Rights Reserved. Used by Permission.

THE GHETTO (TOO SHORT VERSION)
By Todd Shaw/Alfred Eaton/Donny Hathaway/Leroy Hutson
Copyright © 1990 by Don-Pow Music administered be Peer International Corporation. Used by permission. All rights reserved.

GOD'S GIFT
Written by Jean Grae (T. Ibrahim)
Copyright © 2002 Liu Sing Publishing ASCAP
All Rights Reserved. Used by Permission.

HEAVEN ONLY KNOWS
Words and Music by Michael Gomez and Eve Jeffers
© 1999 DEAD GAME PUBLISHING, WHY OH PUBLISHING and BLONDIE ROCKWELL
All Rights for DEAD GAME PUBLISHING and WHY OH PUBLISHING Controlled and Administered by EMI APRIL MUSIC INC.
All Rights Reserved. International Copyright Secured. Used by Permission.

HOW TO ROB
Words and Music by Jean Oliver, Samuel Barnes, Curtis Jackson, Deric Angelettie, Harry Casey and Richard Finch

Copyright © 1999 Sony/ATV Music Publishing LLC, Ekop Publishing LLC, Enot Publishing LLC, 50 Cent Music, EMI Longitude Music, Deric Angeletti Music, Slam U Well Music and Universal Music Corp.
All Rights for Sony/ATV Music Publishing LLC, Ekop Publishing LLC and Enot Publishing LLC Administered by Sony/ATV Music Publishing LLC, 8 Music Square West, Nashville, TN 37203
All Rights for 50 Cent Music Controlled and Administered by Universal Music Corp.
All Rights for Deric Angelettie Music Controlled and Administered by EMI Blackwood Music Inc.
International Copyright Secured. All Rights Reserved.
Contains elements of "I Get Lifted" (Casey/Finch)

I AM I BE
Words and Music by Berry Gordy, Frank E. Wilson, Brenda Holloway, Patrice Holloway, Kelvin Mercer and Vincent Mason
© 1994 JOBETE MUSIC CO., INC., STONE AGATE MUSIC and DAISY AGE MUSIC
All Rights for JOBETE MUSIC CO., INC. and STONE AGATE MUSIC (A Division of JOBETE MUSIC CO., INC.) Controlled and Administered by EMI APRIL MUSIC INC. and EMI BLACKWOOD MUSIC INC.
All Rights Reserved. International Copyright Secured. Used by Permission.

I KNOW YOU GOT SOUL
Words and Music by Eric Barrier, Charles Bobbit, James Brown, Bobby Byrd and William Griffin
Copyright © 1987 UNIVERSAL—SONGS OF POLYGRAM INTERNATIONAL, INC., ROBERT HILL MUSIC, and UNICHAPPELL MUSIC INC.
All Rights for ROBERT HILL MUSIC Controlled and Administered by UNIVERSAL—SONGS OF POLYGRAM INTERNATIONAL, INC.
All Rights Reserved. Used by Permission.

I NEED LOVE
Words and Music by James Todd Smith, Dwayne Simon, Bobby Ervin, Darryl Pierce and Steven Ettinger
Copyright © 1987, 1995 Sony/ATV Music Publishing LLC, LL Cool J Music and Universal Music Corp.
All Rights on behalf of Sony/ATV Music Publishing LLC and LL Cool J Music Administered by Sony/ATV Music Publishing LLC, 8 Music Square West, Nashville, TN 37203
International Copyright Secured. All Rights Reserved.

IMPOSSIBLE
Words and Music by Dennis Coles, Robert Diggs, Lamont Hawkins, Corey Woods and Selwyn Bougard
Copyright © 1997 by Universal Music—Careers, Wu-Tang Publishing, Inc. and Diggs Family Music, Inc.
All Rights for Wu-Tang Publishing, Inc. Administered by Universal Music—Careers
International Copyright Secured. All Rights Reserved.

IN DA CLUB
Words and Music by Curtis Jackson, Andre Young and Michael Elizondo

Copyright © 2003 UNIVERSAL MUSIC CORP., 50 CENT MUSIC, BUG MUSIC-MUSIC OF WINDSWEPT, BLOTTER MUSIC, ELVIS MAMBO MUSIC, WB MUSIC CORP. and AIN'T NOTHIN' BUT FUNKIN' MUSIC
All Rights for 50 CENT MUSIC Controlled and Administered by UNIVERSAL MUSIC CORP.
All Rights for BLOTTER MUSIC and ELVIS MAMBO MUSIC Controlled and Administered by BUG MUSIC-MUSIC OF WINDSWEPT
All Rights for AIN'T NOTHIN' BUT FUNKIN' MUSIC Controlled and Administered by WB MUSIC CORP.
All Rights Reserved. Used by Permission.

INTERNALLY BLEEDING
Written by Immortal Technique
Copyright © 2003
From the Viper Records release, *Revolutionary Vol. 2*
All Rights Reserved. Used by Permission.

JUICY
Words and Music by Sean Combs, Christopher Wallace, Jean Claude Olivier and James Mtume
© 1994 EMI APRIL MUSIC INC., JUSTIN COMBS PUBLISHING COMPANY INC., BIG POPPA MUSIC, JUMPING BEANS SONGS LLC and MTUME MUSIC
All Rights for JUSTIN COMBS PUBLISHING COMPANY INC. and BIG POPPA MUSIC Controlled and Administered by EMI APRIL MUSIC INC.
All Rights Reserved. International Copyright Secured. Used by Permission.
Contains elements of "Juicy Fruit"

KEEP LIVIN
Words and Music by ROBERTA FLACK, CHARLES M. MANN, DONNY HATHAWAY and TSIDI A. IBRAHIM
© 2004 WB MUSIC CORP. (ASCAP), KUUMBA MUSIC (ASCAP) and LIU SING PUBLISHING (ASCAP) All Rights on behalf of Itself and KUUMBA MUSIC Administered by WB MUSIC CORP.
All Rights Reserved. Used by Permission of ALFRED PUBLISHING CO., INC.

KILL THAT NOISE
Written by Shawn Moltke and Marlon Williams
© 1987 CAK Music Publishing, Inc.
All Rights Reserved. Permission Granted.

LADIES FIRST
Words and Music by SHANE FABER, QUEEN LATIFAH and MARK JAMES
Copyright © 1989 WARNER-TAMERLANE PUBLISHING CORP., NOW & THEN MUSIC, WB MUSIC CORP., QUEEN LATIFAH MUSIC INC., FORTY FIVE KING MUSIC, FORKED TONGUE MUSIC and SIMONE JOHNSON PUB. DESIGNEE
All Rights on Behalf of itself and NOW & THEN MUSIC
Administered by WARNER-TAMERLANE PUBLISHING CORP.
All Rights on Behalf of itself, QUEEN LATIFAH MUSIC INC, FORTY FIVE KING MUSIC, FORKED TONGUE MUSIC and SIMONE JOHNSON PUB. DESIGNEE
Administered by WB MUSIC CORP.
All Rights Reserved. Used by Permission of ALFRED PUBLISHING CO., INC.

"the lesson of the falling leaves" from *Good Woman: Poems and a Memoir, 1969–1980.* Copyright © 1987 by Lucille Clifton. Reprinted with the permission of BOA Editions, Ltd., www.boaeditions.org.

THE LIGHT
Words and Music by Lonnie Rashid Lynn, James Yancey, Bobby Caldwell, Norman Harris and Bruce Malament
Copyright © 2000 SONGS OF UNIVERSAL, INC., SENSELESS MUSIC, INC., UNIVERSAL—POLYGRAM INTERNATIONAL PUBLISHING, INC., E.P.C.H.Y. PUBLISHING, BOBBY CALDWELL MUSIC, THE MUSIC FORCE and BENDAN MUSIC
All Rights for SENSELESS MUSIC, INC. Controlled and Administered by SONGS OF UNIVERSAL, INC.
All Rights for E.P.C.H.Y. PUBLISHING Controlled and Administered by UNIVERSAL—POLYGRAM INTERNATIONAL PUBLISHING, INC.
All Rights Reserved. Used by Permission.

LISTENING
Words and Music by Thomas Jones, Phonte Coleman and Patrick Douthit
Copyright © 2003 Imagine Nation Music, Big Pooh Music, Bug Music-Music Of Windswept, It's A Wonderful World Music, Hitco Music, Always Bigger And Better Music and Veoris Music
All Rights for Always Bigger And Better Music, Hitco Music and It's A Wonderful World Music Administered by Bug Music-Songs Of Windswept Pacific
All Rights for Veoris Music, Imagine Nation Music and Big Pooh Music Administered by Bug Music-Music Of Windswept
All Rights Reserved. Used by Permission.

LOVE'S GONNA GET'CHA
Words and Music by Lawrence Parker and Toni Colandreo
Copyright © 1990 by Universal Music—Z Tunes LLC, House Of Fun Music, Inc. and Publisher Unknown
All Rights for House Of Fun Music, Inc. Administered by Universal Music—Z Tunes LLC
International Copyright Secured. All Rights Reserved.

MANIFESTO
Words and Music by Talib Kweli and Tony Cottrell
Copyright © 1998 Songs Of Windswept Pacific, DJ Hi Tek Music Publishing and Pen Skills Music
All Rights Administered by Songs Of Windswept Pacific
All Rights Reserved. Used by Permission.

THE MARCH
Words and Music by Edwin M. Hayes, Jr.
Copyright © 1998
All Rights Reserved. Used by Permission.

MEMORY LANE
Words and Music by Nasir Jones, Peg Barsella and Ruben Wilson
Copyright © 1994 by Ill Will Music, Inc., Skematics Music, Inc. and EMI Unart Catalog, Inc.
All Rights for Ill Will Music, Inc. and Skematics Music, Inc. Administered by Universal Music—Z Tunes LLC
International Copyright Secured. All Rights Reserved.

THE MESSAGE
Written by Sylvia Robinson, Clifton Chase, Melvin Glover, Edward Fletcher
Copyright © 1982 Sugarhill Music
All Rights Reserved. Used by Permission.

A MILLION EYES
Written by Apani Smith
Copyright © 2009 ABMC Muzik Universal Publishing
All Rights Reserved. Permission Granted.

MIND PLAYING TRICKS ON ME
Words and Music by Isaac Hayes, Brad Jordan, Willie Dennis and Doug King
Copyright © 1991 INCENSE PRODUCTIONS, INC. and N-THE-WATER PUBLISHING, INC.
All Rights for INCENSE PRODUCTIONS, INC. Controlled and Administered by IRVING MUSIC, INC.
All Rights Reserved. Used by Permission.

MOMENT OF CLARITY
Words and Music by Shawn Carter and Marshall Mathers
Copyright © 2003 CARTER BOYS PUBLISHING and EIGHT MILE STYLE
All Rights for CARTER BOYS PUBLISHING Controlled and Administered by EMI APRIL MUSIC INC.
All Rights Reserved. International Copyright Secured. Used by Permission.

MY BITCHES
Words and Music by Earl Simmons, Kasseem Dean, Jay Jackson and Darrin Dean
Copyright © 1999 EMI APRIL MUSIC INC., DEAD GAME PUBLISHING, BOOMER X PUBLISHING, INC., SWIZZ BEATZ, RYDE OR DIE PUBLISHING and PUBLISHER UNKNOWN
All Rights for DEAD GAME PUBLISHING Controlled and Administered by EMI APRIL MUSIC INC.
All Rights Reserved. International Copyright Secured. Used by Permission.
Contains elements of "My Niggaz" (Simmons/Dean)

NIGGERS ARE SCARED OF REVOLUTION
Written by Jerome Gilbert Huling
Copyright © 1970 Jerome Gilbert Huling
All Rights Reserved. Permission Granted.

"PHENOMENAL WOMAN"
Copyright © 1978 by MAYA ANGELOU from AND STILL I RISE by Maya Angelou. Used by permission of Random House, Inc.

"PRIVATE SADNESS"
By Robert Kaufman, from THE ANCIENT RAIN: POEMS 1956–1978
Copyright © 1981 by Bob Kaufman.
Reprinted by permission of New Directions Publishing Corp.

PROUD TO BE BLACK
By JOSEPH SIMMONS, DARRYL MCDANIELS and ANDRE A. BROWN

© RABASSE MUSIC, LTD (PRS) and RUSH GROOVE MUSIC (ASCAP)
All Rights Administered by WARNER/CHAPPELL MUSIC LTD
All Rights Reserved.

RESPIRATION
Words and Music by Tony Cottrell and Dante Smith
© 1998 EMI BLACKWOOD MUSIC INC., MEDINA SOUND MUSIC, BUG MUSIC-SONGS
OF WINDSWEPT PACIFIC and DJ HI-TEK MUSIC
All Rights for MEDINA SOUND MUSIC Controlled and Administered by EMI BLACKWOOD
MUSIC INC.
All Rights Reserved. International Copyright Secured.Used by Permission.

THE REVOLUTION WILL NOT BE TELEVISED
Written by Gil Scott-Heron
Used by permission of Bienstock Publishing Company

SATISFIED?
Written by Jean-Jacques Cadet, V. Williams
Copyright © Only Child's Brother's Music/ASCAP/RykoMusic/ASCAP, a div. of EverGreen
Copyrights (Both admin. By ICG)/Ill Mental Music Publishing/BMI.
All rights reserved. Used by permission.

SHADOWS ON THE SUN
Written by Brother Ali for Nafsin Waheedah (ASCAP)
Taken from the album *Shadows On The Sun*
Copyright © 2003 Rhymesayers Entertainment, LLC
All Rights Reserved. Used by Permission.

SHITTY SITUATION
Words and Music by Oscar Jackson P/K/A/ "PARIS"
© 1993 Guerrilla Funk Recordings & Filmworks, LLC
All Rights Reserved. Used by Permission.

TAKE ME
Written by Jean Grae (T. Ibrahim)
Copyright © 2003 Liu Sing Publishing ASCAP
All Rights Reserved. Used by Permission.

THEY REMINISCE OVER YOU (T.R.O.Y.)
Words by COREY BRENT PENN
Music by PETER O. PHILLIPS
© 1992 WB MUSIC CORP. and NESS, NITTY AND CAPONE, INC.
All Rights Administered by WB MUSIC CORP.
All Rights Reserved.

THIS IS WHO I AM
Words and Music by Kasseem Dean, Victor Santiago and Mashonda Tifrere
Copyright © 2003 UNIVERSAL MUSIC CORP., SWIZZ BEATZ, NOTORIOUS K.I.M.
MUSIC and MASHONDA TIFRERE
All Rights for SWIZZ BEATZ Controlled and Administered by UNIVERSAL MUSIC CORP.
All Rights Reserved. Used by Permission.

TIMES ARE GETTIN' ILL
By ROBERT JR. GINYARD
© RABASSE MUSIC, LTD (PRS)
All Rights Administered by WARNER/CHAPPELL MUSIC LTD
All Rights Reserved.

U.N.I.T.Y.
Words and Music by Joe Sample and Dana Owens pka Queen Latifah
(Samples "Message From The Inner City" by Joe Sample)
Copyright © 1993 by Chrysalis Music Ltd. and Queen Latifah Music
All Rights for Chrysalis Music Ltd. in the USA and Canada Administered by Chrysalis Music
All Rights Reserved. Used by Permission.

WHITE AMERICA
Words and Music by Marshall Mathers (BMI), Luis Edgardo Resto (ASCAP), Steven Lee King
(BMI), and Jeffrey Bass (BMI)
Copyright © 2002 by Eight Mile Style, LLC/Martin Affiliated LLC, Jaceff Music LLC/Nueve
Music LLC
Administered by Kobalt Music Publishing America, Inc.

WHITE MAN'Z WORLD
Words and Music by Tupac Shakur and Marvin Harper
Copyright © 1996 SONGS OF UNIVERSAL, INC., JOSHUA'S DREAM MUSIC and SUGE
PUBLISHING
All Rights for JOSHUA'S DREAM MUSIC Controlled and Administered by SONGS OF
UNIVERSAL, INC.
All Rights Reserved. Used by Permission.

WHO PROTECTS US FROM YOU?
Words and Music by Lawrence Parker
Copyright © 1989 by Universal Music—Z Tunes LLC
International Copyright Secured. All Rights Reserved.

WONDER WHY THEY CALL U BYTCH
Words and Music by Tupac Shakur and Johnny Lee Jackson
Copyright © 1996 SONGS OF UNIVERSAL, INC., JOSHUA'S DREAM MUSIC, UNIVER-
SAL MUSIC—MGB SONGS and BLACK HISPANIC MUSIC
All Rights for JOSHUA'S DREAM MUSIC Controlled and Administered by SONGS OF
UNIVERSAL, INC.
All Rights for BLACK HISPANIC MUSIC Controlled and Administered by UNIVERSAL
MUSIC—MGB SONGS
All Rights Reserved. Used by Permission.

Rewind

It was a bright summer Saturday morning. I was upstairs scrubbing the bathroom floor, trying to keep my mother from getting on my case for being lazy. I remember the football-shaped brush moving in small circles over the square white tiles of the floor. I was moving fast because just after lunch I wanted to play stickball with my friends.

Suddenly from the street I heard the sound of screeching tires. Then there were a series of loud crashes. I jumped up and ran down the steps to my front door.

My house was second from the corner of Stillman and Thompson Streets. I hit the door, not breaking stride, and headed down Stillman. Already there was a crowd of people gathered where the car had come to rest, enmeshed in a high, brown wooden fence. But the people weren't focused on the car. Everyone was gathered around a little boy. He had been hit by the car. Part of his head had been smashed in the accident. It was Johnny, a kid who lived on Seybert Street, one block away.

Johnny had been eating an ice cream cone. The blood and the melting ice cream mixed to form a most curious pink river that was slowly winding its way through the crevices in the cement to the sea of black asphalt that was the street. But Johnny did not die. Weeks later, I saw Johnny sitting on his steps with a cast on his head. He looked like a Spanish conquistador.

Months after that, Johnny started coming out to play again. But he was different. There was an uncertain smile flashing. This new Johnny was nervous and unpredictable. And the scar on the top of his head reminded everyone that he was indeed different now. I can only remember him after the accident. When I hear his voice in my head, it's affected, too loud, and precise.

After the accident, Johnny never made sense. He would string words to-gether in no apparent order. He would use incredibly long and obscure words in sentences that came to no conclusion and seemed to have no meaning. Johnny would walk up to you and say something like, "Did you know that the plastericized notary of signatures is only faster than the supernova in perpetu-ity?" You had to decide whether to laugh or just act as if you knew what he was talking about.

This was in North Philadelphia, in the density of blackness. In the life. We accepted him anyway. We loved Johnny. Nobody teased him. Well, actually, we started calling him the Professor.

There were many nights when we sat on the front steps in the ghetto shad-ows and listened to the Professor pontificate. Johnny tried to articulate, even when his head was a jumble of parts improperly put back together, because it was an essential element in his fight for humanity. And he gravitated to words because words demonstrate to the world that you are a human being. Not a savage or an animal. Words spoken, words written, affirm and give voice to our dreams, our imaginations.

But the Professor took it even further. Perhaps in an instinctive and uncon-scious effort to compensate for the disability suffered from the accident, he somehow deduced that the bigger the words, the more intelligent he would be perceived. In his relearning process, the Professor memorized the words straight from the dictionary.

Unfortunately, the memorization of words, without careful thought to their meanings and without an understanding of the contextual impact of sentence structure, had the opposite effect. It made us all look at him and feel sad.

How much pain he must have suffered. How confused he must have been in that world. He tried with everything he had to sound intelligent. And he almost did. You could talk with the Professor for a long time without real-izing that you had no understanding of what he was talking about.

I think a lot about the Professor now as I write about rap music. Rap/poets are engaged in a desperate, perhaps even an unconscious attempt to provide a contemporary humanity for marginalized people. Particularly black folks. Instead of three-dollar words that make no sense when strung together like Johnny the Professor might use, rap/poets reach past the conventional lan-guage, past the conventional treatment of subject matter, past the conven-tional analysis of social problems to make sense of our world—to say: "I am. I exist. You cannot forget about me." And to this I would add that rap/poets also reveal to us the consequences of our (parents'/society's) weaknesses.

To some in the world outside hip hop, rap/poets sound like the Professor did to me: sad, unfortunate, miseducated and misguided souls, pontificating on non-understandable subjects. But on reflection, as I considered the high quality of some rap/poems, I began to think differently about the Professor. I think now that we simply did not understand the Professor's language, his system of meaning. He was Signifyin(g) on us—deriving his own power from the insertion of *his* language into our world. The Professor would sometimes look at us with a smirk on his face as if we were the ones who were lost.

This is precisely the position rap/poets take with respect to the mainstream world. They talk around, over, and through the world they oppose. They collect checks as proof of their stealth. This does not, however, change the fact that those same checks quantify the level of exploitation and manipulation exerted on this art by the music industry.

But Johnny the Professor and rap/poets have at least two things in common. They all use words that make sense to some and are meaningless to others. And they all expend a great deal of energy to do a simple thing: speak.

1

Say What?

It must first be said that this book is focused on the "speech" of rap: the narrative and the poetic. It has little concern for all that is popular about rap music. The pop culture icons of rap, from 50 Cent to Lil Wayne, are not the subjects of this discussion. While Ja Rule, Lil Jon, Soulja Boy, and other annually appearing rap stars provide rap music with new listeners and instant reinvigoration, they do not define the path of our quest. This is not to say that each of them hasn't produced quality poems. But it is to say that in this book, I tried to be as unmoved by popular iconic hoopla as was humanly possible.

There is, instead, pulsating at the core of rap, a literary heart that burns to be recognized. While it is true that whether we are "In Da Club," "Down with OPP," or head bopping to "Crank That," popular rap commands much of the attention. It is truer still that popular rap music is under the tight control of the music industry. And what is most often heard (on MTV, BET, and local commercial radio) is not even slightly representative of the depth and dimension of the poetry of rap.

I am, however, interested in the overarching embrace of hip hop culture. Hip hop has a history, a storied evolution that is well documented by various scholars.[1] But most folks, both streetwise and scholarly, attribute the term "hip hop" to DJ Kool Herc—one of the seminal pioneers along with Afrika Bambaataa.

When most people define hip hop, they generally talk about its components. They begin by saying that hip hop is a culture that is composed of rapping, breaking, graffiti, deejaying, and so forth.

One of the great voices of hip hop, KRS-One, in his recording of the rap/poem "HipHop Knowledge," includes a short interview at its conclusion. It is there we find his now famous statement: "Rap music, is something we do,

1

but HIP-HOP, is something we live. And we look at hip-hop, in its 9 elements; which is breaking, emceeing, graffiti art, deejaying, beatboxing, street fashion, street language, street knowledge, and street entrepreneurialism—trade and business. . . . We come from the uhh the root of, of DJ Kool Herc, who originated hip-hop in the early 70s and then Afrika Bambaataa and Zulu Nation (mmhmm) who instigated something called The Infinity Lessons and added consciousness to hip-hop, and then Grandmaster Flash with the invention of the mixer, on to Run DMC and then myself. . . . All of this, goes to the idea of LIVING this culture out and taking responsibility for how it looks and acts in society."[2]

So in general, definitions of hip hop take shape around its pieces. But it is in the explication of the parts of hip hop culture that we generally come to feel its power and complexity. The relationship between the components of hip hop is a profoundly spiritual one, as KRS-One reveals.

Sometimes this definition is augmented by an accounting of the sociological and economic conditions that created the environment into which hip hop was born. For example, Tricia Rose explicates in her book *Black Noise* how the post-industrial realities of urban America, particularly in the Northeast, had rendered young black and Latino men as less than viable, disenfranchised "problems."[3] Hip hop, then, is often defined as simply a response to this bleak reality.

I want to offer a definition of hip hop that has embedded in it the multicultural, progressively political, and open-minded sensibilities that provide rap/poetry with a natural home. For the duration of this discussion, *hip hop is the world, the culture that envelopes rap (including rap/poetry and the music).* Although there are strongly negative impulses circulating within this cultural reality, I understand hip hop culture as *one that is politically oppositional to an imagined dominant majority (read white), overtly racialized (read African American), heteronormative, youth centered, competitive, egalitarian, and global.* I will come back to this definition because it informs the way I interact and "read" rap/poetry.

I think of rap/poetry as the literary manifestation of this culture. The other "components" provide its visual (graffiti), dance (breaking, locking, etc.), music (deejaying), language, and style. All of these components (whether you list four, nine, or fifteen) function together as a trope of popular culture, but the *poetry* of hip hop extends beyond that boundary and into the embrace of literature. The poetry in rap is poetry because it emanates from the African American community in the same way that all of the poetry that came before rap did. It conforms to the structure, historical trajectory, and evolution of African American poetry. When I use the term *rap*, I am talking generally about the totality of the expression: music, performance, and poetry. But my primary focus here, as I've made clear, is strictly on the poetry in the form I call rap/poetry.

Here's the gift: rap/poetry is the emergent African American literary form of the postmodern age. Yes, it has it roots in African and African American oral tradition, and it has slowly evolved from the playground to the lips of actors, politicians, and teachers. But its bloodline can also be traced back through the pages of words set down by African American culture's most significant poets. Placing rap/poetry within this historical and literary context moves us far past the commonly heard rap song and the usual lip service paid to the poetic skills of popular rappers.

Most of the important rap/poets write their words first as poems. This is important to note because literary talent is not readily acknowledged when it emanates from inner-city ghettos. It is instinctive for popular media to appreciate the musical, rhythmic qualities of a rap song and completely overlook its message and poetic construction. It continues to surprise me when people who have only a cursory understanding of rap talk about rappers as if they are illiterate. People who create rap/poems—even not very good ones—are seldom illiterate.

If you are to take rap seriously, you must take the rap/poet seriously. We must privilege the poet's potential and capacity for intention when it is apparent that a rap/poem demonstrates insight, power, or a keen observation. It is my experience that people are more likely to dismiss quality as accidental when it comes to rap/poetry than attribute it to the intellectual and artistic mastery of the rapper.

There are those who believe that rap, like any form of popular music, is a blend of music and words that are inseparable. This assumption obscures the central power of rap, which to me resides not at all in the music but, rather, in the words. I want to *liberate* the poetry of rap—the literature of hip hop—from the stereotyped expectations of their function as "songs."

In this book, I claim that the poetry of rap constitutes a whole, and that the music, or the beat of rap, is an addition to that whole. This revised notion of rap is a challenge to musicians and other people who have always only viewed rap as a form of music. More to the point, I argue that *when it comes to rap, the words are more important than the music.* And to further complicate this challenge, I am also suggesting that, in order to deal with the literary achievements of a given rap/poem, we must dismiss the actual sound of the poet's voice.

Listening to Wu-Tang Clan's RZA recite his part of the rap/poem "Impossible" is entirely different than reading it.

> Fusion of the five elements, to search for the higher intelligence
> Women walk around celibate, livin irrelevant
> The most benevolent king, communicatin through your dreams
> Mental pictures been painted, Allah's heard and seen
> everywhere, throughout your surroundin atmosphere
> Troposphere, thermosphere, stratosphere
> Can you imagine from one single idea, everything appeared here
> Understanding makes my truth, crystal clear
> Innocent black immigrants locked in housing tenements
> Eighty-five percent tenants depend on welfare recipients

Anyone who is familiar with RZA's deep, sonorous, driving voice would probably choose to listen rather than read this poem. But this poem, with its charismatic internal rhyme scheme, does not need his voice or the external music. It reveals its complexity of image, texture, and meaning very effectively, even deftly, through the use of language.

RZA's voice, like Chuck D's or Ice T's or even Pharoahe Monch's, grabs you like a strong hand. If it moves, you move. But could you simply read it? Can we take the charismatic RZA out of the equation and put him in the place of the poet? Can he survive the scrutiny the page brings with it? I believe he can.

There is no question that Chuck D's voice or KRS-One's or MC Lyte's or Bahamadia's has something to do with their success as poets. The performance of the poem has tremendous impact on our capacity to hear and embrace its message. But can we look at a rap/poem devoid of the audible voice and the attending music? I suggest we can.

When the rap/poet I Self Devine visited my class, I had a message for him and for my students. Here was a true poet standing before them. If you discount him simply because he is an underground rap artist, you betta recognize: he is a poet. His poetic brilliance rises from the page like heat waves. When I Self and many other equally talented rap/poets decide to stop producing rap CDs, they should create publishing houses to produce their work as literature.

The best of the rap/poets are very conscious of their literary realities, conscious of the writing process itself. This excerpt from "I Know You Got Soul," by Rakim of the group Eric B. and Rakim, reveals the poetic mind:

> I start to think
> and then I sink
> into the paper
> like I was ink
> when I'm writin
> I'm trapped in between

> the lines
> I escape when I finish
> the rhyme

This is a particularly important stanza because it occurred so early (1986) in the development of rap as the literary manifestation of hip hop culture. Rakim's rap/poem articulates the intellectual, metaphysical, and literary process that poets experience when they create. Rakim, of course, would go on to become one of the most significant rap/poets in the history of hip hop.

Another skilled rap/poet, Talib Kweli, writes in "Manifesto":

> Every MC grab a pen
> and write some conscious lyrics
> to tell the children
> I'll say it again,
> every MC find you a pen
> And drop some conscious shit
> for our children

Examples abound of rap/poets who openly write about writing. In "The 6th Sense," Common writes, "[I] Escape through rhythms in search of peace and wisdom / Raps are smoke signals letting the streets know I'm with 'em." Rap/poet Immortal Technique in his "Internally Bleeding" poem writes: "And this is prophecy, the words that I speak from my lungs / The severed head of John the Baptist speaking in tongues / Like 'Che Guevara' my soliloquies speak to a gun / Paint in slow motion like trees that reach for the sun."

Consider the intense and direct understanding expressed by Brother Ali in "Shadows on the Sun":

> I keep an eye on heaven and a ear to the street
> And spread a thick layer of blood, sweat and tears on the beats
> My brain rests upon the hip-hop lexicon
> That I acquired in the decade of work that people slept upon
> I don't rap, I recite the prayers of the inner soul
> Of the slave ships' human cargo

Rap/poetry offers the flesh, the blood, the ideas, the shame, and the beauty of the inner city. It communicates the struggling, angry, and glorious world of besieged urban African Americans. This is a world that had been waiting for hip hop to arrive. Hip hop—the music and the life—is the messenger. And rap/poetry is the message.

As a writer, I was drawn to rap nearly from the moment I was introduced to it in the late 1970s. I immediately felt that it was perhaps the greatest literary discovery that African American culture had ever seen, on a par with Gutenberg's moveable-type press. It offered a freedom of speech to voices (namely young black inner-city youth) that had been completely shut out of other kinds of public or literary discourse. I realize that hip hop culture was founded and nourished by people from all cultural and racial identities. Dance, dress, graffiti, speech, and even music have many contributors of note outside the African American community. But rap/poetry is derived almost entirely from African American literary tradition, which of course has its own history and relationships with many cultures.

As I listened ever more closely, it was clear that there was indeed a connection between rap/poets and the historical continuum of African American poetry—a psychic and perhaps even spiritual relationship, if you will. Rap/poets seemed to be saddled with the same demand that African American poets had been since slavery, to provide a functional, "impactful" influence in the reality of black Americans. By "impactful," I mean to say that black poets have always set out—from the earliest poetic expression—to light a path to dignity, power, self-identification, self-determination, defiance, and survival. From James Weldon Johnson to Maya Angelou. From Robert Hayden to Sekou Sundiata. From Phyllis Wheatley to Sonia Sanchez.

African American culture flows through time like a river. It has many tributaries, but poetry is the source of its momentum. In this way, poets like Maya Angelou, Langston Hughes, Yusef Komunyakaa, Claude McKay, Amiri Baraka, Haki Madhubuti, Nikki Giovanni, Ted Joans, Bob Kaufman, Quincy Troupe, Countee Cullen, Rita Dove, and even Sterling Brown are all connected to contemporary rap/poets.

When I first heard KRS-One's "Who Protects Us from You?" which includes the following,

> You were put here to protect us
> But who protects us from you?
> Every time you say "That's illegal"
> Doesn't mean that that's true (Uh-huh)
> Your authority's never questioned
> No-one questions you
> If I hit you I'll be killed
> But you hit me? I can sue (Order! Order!)
> Lookin' through my history book
> I've watched you as you grew
> Killin' blacks and callin' it the law
> (Bo! Bo! Bo!) And worshipping Jesus too
> There was a time when a black man
> Couldn't be down wit' your crew (Can I have a job please?)

Now you want all the help you can get
Scared? Well ain't that true (You goddamn right)
You were put here to protect us
But who protects us from you?
Or should I say, who are you protecting?
The rich? the poor? Who?

I couldn't help thinking about Langston Hughes's "Who but the Lord?":

I looked and I saw
That man they call the Law.
He was coming
Down the street at me!
I had visions in my head
Of being laid out cold and dead,
Or else murdered
By the third degree.

I said, O Lord, if you can,
Save me from that man!
Don't let him make a pulp out of me!
But the Lord he was not quick.
The Law raised up his stick
And beat the living hell
Out of me!

Now I do not understand
Why God don't protect a man
From police brutality.
Being poor and black,
I've no weapon to strike back
So who but the Lord
Can protect me?
We'll see.

The sense of threat and danger the police represent is present in both works, as is the idea of religious hypocrisy. Despite the decades that elapsed between these two poems, it is both depressing and profound that the concerns of the two poets about the condition of urban black America reflects little difference. It is also central to my discussion that Langston Hughes was one of America's greatest poets. So the fact that a rap/poet, in this case KRS-One, would follow a form so naturally indicates that this expression comes from the same origins.

Here is another example that demonstrates the direct link between rap/poets of the present and poets of the past. When I first heard Aceyalone's "The March," which includes the following lines,

> I was born in a concrete jungle
> and I learned to make my own way (learned to make my own way)
> I was raised by streets and the beats
> and the books and crooks of L.A.
> I was taken by the power of the word
> and I had a whole lot to say (had a whole lot to say)
> And I vowed, always to move the crowd
> and leave em in disarray
> Cause I live by the word AND I die by the sword
> These here are strange days AND we here are strong
> We live by the sword AND we die by the slug
> This here is war AND this here is love
> Soldiers are marching in
> And they're going to battle again
> Somebody's going to win
> and somebody will lose—and that's the truth!

I couldn't help but think of Bob Kaufman's "Private Sadness":

> Sitting here alone, in peace
> With my private sadness
> Bared of the acquirements
> Of the mind's eye
> Vision reversed, upended,
> Seeing only the holdings
> Inside the walls of me,
> Feeling the roots that bind me,
> To this mere human tree
> Thrashing to free myself,
> Knowing the success
> Of these burstings
> Shall be measured
> By the fury
> Of the fall
> To eternal peace
> The end of All.

While Kaufman's poem is one of internal inventory, of a man at counsel with himself, and Aceyalone's eye focuses as much on the external as the internal, it is the sense of disconnection, disaffection, and struggle that connects these poems. And perhaps more significantly, both poems provide words to describe the melancholy that pervades the lives of many African American men.

Or consider the similarity in theme and nuance between Claude McKay's "The White City" and excerpts from rap/poems by Tupac Shakur, Talib Kweli, and Outkast. In Tupac's "White Man'z World," we are not privileged with the richly foreboding description of McKay. We are instead told about the consequences. And these are underscored by the realization that Tupac's world and McKay's are constructed and colored by the same power of race. The image of the city dominates in these poems much as it does in all rap/ poetry. But in excerpts from Kweli and Outkast, the shadow of whiteness and its oppressive manifestations creep over the terrain. Each poet interprets the resulting sense of isolation and injustice that the urban environment creates. First, "The White City":

> I will not toy with it nor bend an inch.
> Deep in the secret chambers of my heart
> I muse my life-long hate, without flinch
> I bear it nobly as I live my part.
> My being would be a skeleton, a shell,
> If this dark Passion that fills my every mood,
> And makes my heaven in the white world's hell,
> Did not forever feed me vital blood.
> I see the mighty city through a mist—
> The strident trains that speed the goaded mass,
> The poles and spires and towers vapor-kissed,
> The fortressed port through which the great ships pass,
> The tides, the wharves, the dens I contemplate,
> Are sweet like wanton loves because I hate.

And Tupac Shakur's "White Man'z World":

> Bein born with less I must confess only adds on to the stress
> Two gunshots to my homie's head, dyed in his vest
> Shot him to death and left him bleedin for his family to see
> I pass his casket gently askin, is there heaven for G's?
> My homeboy's doin life, his baby momma be stressin
> Sheddin tears when her son, finally asks that question
> Where my daddy at? Mama why we live so poor?
> Why you cryin? Heard you late night through my bedroom door
> Now do you love me mama? Whitey keep on callin me nigga?
> Get my weight up with my hate and pay 'em back when I'm bigger
> And still thuggin in this jail cell, missin my block

Hearin brothers screamin all night, wishin they'd stop
Proud to be black but why we act like we don't love ourselves
Don't look around busta (you sucka) check yourselves
Know what it MEANS to be black, whether a man or girl
We still strugglin, in this white man's world

And here is Talib Kweli's contribution to the rap/poem "Respiration" by Blackstar:

Breathin in deep city breaths, sittin on shitty steps
we stoop to new lows, hell froze the night the city slept
The beast crept through concrete jungles
communicatin with one another
And ghetto birds where waters fall
from the hydrants to the gutters
The beast walk the beats, but the beats we be makin
You on the wrong side of the track, lookin visibly shaken
Taken them plungers, plungin to death that's painted by the numbers
with Krylon applied pressure, cats is playin God
but havin children by a lesser baby mother but fuck it
we played against each other like puppets, swearin you got pull
when the only pull you got is the wool over your eyes
Gettin knowledge in jail like a blessing in disguise
Look in the skies for God, what you see besides the smog
is broken dreams flying away on the wings of the obscene

This rap/poem, which uses a variety of poetic techniques, takes us even deeper into McKay's white city—at least the lives of black people there. The lives described all exist within the context of whiteness. "Ghetto birds," "beasts," and "broken dreams" are the reality of this world.

Outkast's "The Art of Storytelling Pt. 1" and McKay's "The White City" may seem like an unlikely pairing. But as I explored the sentiment of this rap/poem and thought about the deep sadness of McKay's poem, it seemed only fitting to present the comparison here:

Three in the morning yawnin dancin under street lights
We chillin like a villain and a nigga feelin right
in the middle of the ghetto on the curb, but in spite
all of the bullshit we on our back starin at the stars above
(aww man) Talkin bout what we gonna be when we grow up
I said what you wanna be, she said, "Alive" (hmm)
It made me think for a minute, then looked in her eyes
I coulda died, time went on, I got grown

The line "I said what you wanna be, she said, 'Alive'" floored me the first time I heard it. It is the sad answer to the reality of life in the city: a place that for both poets—whatever else it is—threatens and stymies young lives. It expresses the recognition that the only way to beat the dangers that lurked and to have the chance at escape, the opportunity to have a better life, was simply to live. To be "Alive."

Then there is this first stanza of Maya Angelou's "Phenomenal Woman":

> I walk into a room
> Just as cool as you please,
> And to a man,
> The fellows stand or
> Fall down on their knees.
> Then they swarm around me,
> A hive of honey bees.
> I say,
> It's the fire in my eyes,
> And the flash of my teeth,
> The swing in my waist,
> And the joy in my feet.
> I'm a woman
> Phenomenally.
> Phenomenal woman,
> That's me.

The reverberations of this poem can be found in nearly every female rap/poet from Lauryn Hill to Rah Digga, and notably in Queen Latifah's (and Monie Love's) classic rap/poem "Ladies First":

> Who said the ladies couldn't make it, you must be blind
> If you don't believe, well here, listen to this rhyme
> Ladies first, there's no time to rehearse
> I'm divine and my mind expands throughout the universe
> A female rapper with the message to send the
> Queen Latifah is a perfect specimen

Indeed, in rap/poetry, perhaps more than in other areas of artistic expression, women have had to defend their humanity. In fact, it is the poetic expression of African American women that has, through time, forced the culture to create, recognize, and accept ever more accurate portrayals of themselves. Many male rap/poets have contributed to a savaging of women (black women in particular), sometimes descending into unrestrained and unapologetic misogyny. Women rap/poets have generally—even in this sexist environment that demands certain undermining hypersexual self-representations—responded with the same fierceness that their sister poets of the past have. Their rap/poems fight back, create personas, explore desires, and reveal truths. We will talk more about this later.

At its best, rap/poetry functions very much for hip hop the way traditional poetry does for mainstream culture. That is, it attempts to establish, articulate, and maintain a value system. It is the nature of the poet to reflect a culture's qualities and struggles, whatever they are, back to the source of the culture's origin. At its best, the poetry identifies and contextualizes all that is true about a people and their ways. At its worst, it is subservient to the most negative instincts, urges, and qualities of our society. At its worst, rap/poetry undermines even hip hop culture's value system.

As I've said, rap/poetry is a progression on the continuum of African American literature. A review of the evolution of African American poetry leads one directly to the gates of rap. Beginning with what editor Dudley Randall in *The Black Poets* called the "folk secular,"[4] work like "Raise a Ruckus To-night" (which actually predates any formal publication of poetry by African Americans) could easily be heard in a contemporary rap/poem:

> Two liddle Niggers all dressed in white, (Raise a ruckus to-night)
> Want to go to Heaben on de tail of a kite. (Raise a ruckus to-night)
> De kite string broke; dem Niggers fell; (Raise a ruckus to-night)
> Whar dem Niggers go, I hain't gwineter tell. (Raise a ruckus to-night)

Rap/poetry is a direct descendent of "Raise a Ruckus." It carries the history of storytelling in verse that has been essential for African American sanity. Rap is a literary art that is forged from need. The need is self-expression, the need to say: "I am. I exist, and this is what I think."

Think about it this way: if you were a fourteen-year-old black boy and you were interested in language, words, and poetry, who would be your contemporary role models? The rap/poets. Who else has visibility as wordsmiths? Who else commands respect as poets/griots/storytellers on the streets? Our youth know precious little about the African American literary poets who struggled to write and publish in America. Our system of education largely overlooks the poetic contributions of contemporary poets of color. Even in my class of graduate students and upper-class undergraduates, precious few have ever read an entire book of poetry by any poet of color, much less by an African American. Said another way, how many living, publishing African American male poets can you name? A posthumous book of poems by rapper Tupac Shakur sold more copies than a book by the living National Book Award–winning poet Yusef Komunyakaa in 2001.

A close review of the poems themselves (which is what this book intends to do) will reveal an incredible degree of sophistication, knowledge, understanding, and compassion present in this expression. This book will, of course, also engage the ignorant, profane, obscene, misogynist, violent, and angry nature of the "I" in the "I am" of rap/poetry. That part is sad but real. More importantly, it is the nature of poetry, since poetry as a literary art form is the form of choice for the expression of emotional feelings, dreams, and desires.

As you read this book, you will find careful consideration of the components of an effective rap/poem. We will examine the language, flow, imagery, meaning, saturation, and texture, as well as the innovative and charismatic power of the best of rap/poetry. It is my hope that you will begin to appreciate the intellect and aesthetical instincts that drive the best of this poetic expression. The fundamental point is that if we engage in an appropriate critical analysis of rap/poetry, the strengths and weaknesses of any given rap/poem will be revealed. It is the best way I know to engage in a discussion about the qualities and highest aspirations of this art.

NOTES

1. There are a number of excellent books about the history of hip hop. One of the best is Jeff Chang's *Can't Stop Won't Stop* (St. Martin's, 2005). There is also *Rap Attack 3* (Serpent's Tail, 1999) by David Toop, *Black Noise* (Wesleyan, 1994) by Tricia Rose, and *Hip Hop America* (Penguin, 1993) by Nelson George, just to name a few.

2. KRS-One, "HipHop Knowledge," *The Sneak Attack* (2001).

3. Tricia Rose documents this reality very well in *Black Noise*.

4. Dudley Randall, ed., *The Black Poets* (Bantam, 1971).

2

A Matter of Life: A Brief Discussion

A review of books on the art and craft of poetry unfortunately reveals no perfect way to define poetry. So instead of one definition, we have resorted to a quilt of interconnected, synergistic definitions. The first supposes that poetry is like a mirror. A reflection. An attempt to get at the truth of oneself and the world that surrounds the poet. It is what stares back. The poet is caught in the act of trying to get as close as one can to the actual truth. The poet functions as a mirror, a reflection of the people and their concerns, from which the poet came. This reflection is conveyed in the natural language of those people. By natural language, I mean the language that most accurately reflects the truths, rhythms, traditions, and potential of those people. Form is a deeply embedded manifestation of cultural rhythm. Iambic pentameter, for example, may be the way we talk sometimes. At other times, our rhythm is iambic hexameter. Both forms exist already inside us.

But is the sonnet a natural form of expression? Haiku? In some cultural realities, they may be as natural as breathing. But they may also be inventions, constructions that caught the ear or the eye. It is somewhat difficult to imagine that there was once a time when haiku was as popular in Japan as rap is now in America.

As proof of the difficulty of defining poetry, poets often use language as abstract and expansive and yet as precise as their work itself. African American poet Audre Lorde wrote: "Poetry is not only dream and vision; it is the skeleton architecture of our lives. It lays the foundations for a future of change, a bridge across our fears of what has never been before."[1] Mexican poet Octavio Paz wrote: "Poetry belongs to all epochs: it is man's natural form of expression."[2] African American poet Lucille Clifton points out: "Poetry is a matter of life, not just a matter of language."[3]

15

Contemplating the entry of rap/poetry into the American literary milieu brings to mind the ways in which poetic expression always appears in response to history. "Every age has its own poetry, in every age the circumstances of history choose a nation, a race, a class to take up the torch by creating situations that can be expressed or transcended only through poetry," wrote French philosopher Jean-Paul Sartre in "Orphée Noir."[4] The volumes of poetry that now routinely erupt from the world's urban centers, labeled in the popular media as rap, actually reach a level of insight, magic, and power that just might reveal rap/poetry to be the "chosen" art Sartre was talking about.

Rap/poetry has become the form of expression of choice for those who stand in opposition to dominant powers throughout the world. In many ways, it works the way poetic expression has always worked. While we think of poetry as an art form used by the elite, it is actually much more immediate and functional to the common folk. One need only consider the role of poetry in the African American civil rights struggle.

Reading Henry Louis Gates Jr.'s *Figures in Black*, I was at once and for always struck by this passage:

> No, blacks could not achieve any true presence by speaking, since their "African"-informed English seemed to have only underscored their status as *sui generis*, as distinct in spoken language use as in their "black" color. If blacks were to signify as full members of the Western human community, they would have to do so in their writings.[5]

Later Gates says: "Literacy—the literacy of formal writing—was both a technology and a commodity. It was a commodity with which the African's right to be considered a human being could be traded."[6] These ideas imbue the "desire to write," to express oneself on the part of black people, with a special value. Perhaps it is at the top of the list of essentials. To be black and to be silent is tantamount to surrendering to the alternative: the non-understandable other.

We begin this conversation about poetry by speaking about its power and significance in a political context, as demonstrated in Langston Hughes's poetry, for example. But poetry reaches way beyond the political. We hold the poet to a certain expectation that he or she will provide us with something we have never seen before that is both beautiful and meaningful. That is, the poet will give us his or her unique truth.

Part of the aesthetic of literary poetry is that the poem can be about something as small and concrete as a moth or something as big and intangible as love or God. The really strong poems can be about both at the same time. It may not seem that each poem is always unique, since literary poetry has trends and genres and common themes, but poetry can never be great unless it tells a truth—coming from the mind of the author, based on the tools and structures of language, and used in a unique way.

In *Western Wind*, Frederick Nims captures the components of poetry quite well. After he makes clear that verse and poetry are two separate things ("Verse is any singsong with rhythm and rhyme"), he writes:

> The nature of poetry follows from our own human nature. The main divisions are organized as we ourselves are. Human experience begins when the senses give us:
>
> (1)
> IMAGES of ourself or of the world outside. These images arouse
> (2)
> EMOTIONS, which (with their images) we express in
> (3)
> WORDS, which are physically produced and have
> (4)
> SOUND, which comes to our ear riding the air on waves of
> (5)
> RHYTHM. The whole process, from the beginning, is fostered and overseen by an organizing
> (6)
> MIND, acting with the common sense of our everyday life, even when dealing with the uncommon sense of dreams or visions.[7]

These same essential elements of poetry can be found, with some significant additions, in rap. It is also true that some rap is more akin to verse than poetry. But it is my contention that the vast majority of rap/poetry conforms to most known notions of Western poetry.

But we won't race to this conclusion. Instead, we intend to examine the literary qualities of rap in a multifaceted way. Form, meaning, and other traditional and nontraditional evaluative mechanisms have been employed to light our way.

The craft of the poet, the forms and challenges of prosody, must be considered when reading any poetry, and they have been in this endeavor as well. But because rap/poetry exists within the nature of an African American literary tradition, there are special concerns we must address, particularly the traditional function of poetry in African American culture. I have come to believe that being oppressed and using poetry as a weapon against the oppressor or those who aid in one's marginalization is natural although often overlooked.

What if, on some of those hot summer nights sitting on the stoop, we had probed the Professor's multisyllabic rantings? What if we had asked what he truly meant to say? What if his language was shrouded from us because of us and not him?

NOTES

1. Audre Lorde, *Sister Outsider* (Crossing Press, 1984), ch. 3.

2. Octavio Paz, *The Bow and the Lyre*, trans. Ruth L. C. Simms (1967; University of Texas Press, 1973), ch. 4.

3. Lucille Clifton, as quoted by Mickey Pearlman in *Listen to Their Voices* (Norton, 1993), ch. 9.

4. Jean-Paul Sartre, "Orphée Noir," introduction to *Anthologie de la Nouvelle Poésie Nègre et Malgache*, ed. Léopold Sédar Senghor (1948).

5. Henry Louis Gates Jr., *Figures in Black* (Oxford University Press, 1987), 6.

6. Gates, *Figures in Black*, 11.

7. Frederick Nims, *Western Wind* (Random House, 1983).

3

From the Streets: Coloring the Multicultural Black

In order to penetrate the code of rap, one must adjust to the cultural perspective of the speakers themselves. This, in fact, is the first and largest barrier for the general public to overcome. Rap represents a vaguely familiar, opposing force to society's norms. And it does so proudly. It flows directly from the explosive period of the Black Arts Movement (BAM). Yes, it has its folkloric and historical literary connections (as I have briefly noted), and it conforms in a general way to traditional expectations of poetry, but its true antecedents can be found in the fiery, unflinching, and angry voices of the black poets that shaped the posture of African Americans during the 1960s and 1970s.

To advocate Black Power and various forms of Black Nationalism, those poets had to construct and legitimize the territory that existed outside of whiteness. The Black Arts poets and writers tried to unearth the roots of whiteness and ideas of white supremacy that were deeply embedded in the African American consciousness. They tried—and succeeded to a large extent—to establish new criteria for effectiveness in black expression. No longer were white critics considered the ultimate arbiters of African American excellence. The BAM theorists and artists demanded that oppositionality be a given in work written for black patrons. To hell with the white audiences altogether.

This movement was fundamentally different from other literary periods that predated it, like the Harlem Renaissance of the 1920s. The Harlem Renaissance had its share of anger, but that discontent was, for the most part, smoothed out by a sense of optimism for the future and a desire to prove once and for all that black artists could produce and compete on a level with white artists. It reflected the feelings of African Americans that better days were ahead.

But by the time the BAM came into being, much, if not all, of that optimism had dissipated. African Americans were tired of being told to be patient in their struggle for equality. They had fought in three significant wars, had put shoulder to wheel in the great growth of this country, and still they were marginal, not whole people in nearly every facet of daily public life.

So the poetry that erupted from the hearts of those poets of the Black Arts Movement systematically challenged everything. It stood up against the order and façade of a dominant white cultural imperative and forced it to accept the presence and power of African American culture. The culture and the poetry demanded it and threatened revolution as the stick that would move the mule of oppression. These word songs reverberated throughout urban and rural black America. They fused with the courage and fortitude of Martin Luther King Jr., Malcolm X, and others and were forged in black brilliance with the militancy of Black Power.

Those poets—including Nikki Giovanni, Sonia Sanchez, Carolyn Rodgers, Haki Madhubuti, Amiri Baraka, Askia Muhammad Toure, Larry Neal, Quincy Troupe, and countless others both widely and locally known—were at the very vanguard of both the BAM and the Black Power movements. Indeed the art and the politics were inextricably woven together.[1]

And the poems these poets produced were nothing like the poems that came before them. The idea of a black aesthetic had emerged, and many of the conventions of Western poetics were either discarded or disfigured. This new aesthetic placed purpose first in the creation of art. And the purpose of art was the liberation of black people from the oppressive images, stereotypes, identities, and constructions that were the tools of white racism. There were many approaches to this objective, but there was an expectation emanating from BAM believers that there was a "positive" art and a "negative" or counterrevolutionary art. A Western "art for art's sake" attitude was unacceptable, as was any work that seemed oblivious or overly conciliatory to the dominant culture.

An excerpt from Amiri Baraka's "Black Art" sets the table perfectly:

> Poems are bullshit unless they are
> teeth or trees or lemons piled
> on a step. Or black ladies dying
> of men leaving nickel hearts
> beating them down. Fuck poems
> and they are useful, wd they shoot
> come at you, love what you are,
> breathe like wrestlers, or shudder
> strangely after pissing. We want live

words of the hip world live flesh &
coursing blood. Hearts Brains
Souls splintering fire. We want poems
like fists beating niggers out of Jocks
or dagger poems in the slimy bellies
of the owner-jews. Black poems to
smear on girdlemamma mulatto bitches
whose brains are red jelly stuck
between 'lizabeth taylor's toes. Stinking
Whores! We want "poems that kill."
Assassin poems, Poems that shoot
guns. Poems that wrestle cops into alleys
and take their weapons leaving them dead
with tongues pulled out and sent to Ireland.

The genetic code for the birth of rap/poetry resides here in this single poem. It is a translation for the current defense of rap/poets responding to would-be censors: "I'm just keepin' it real." The poem "Black Art" offers its reader specific qualities of the successful black poem. Of course, by the end of the Black Arts period, none of these qualities would be acceptable to the emerging American preoccupation with technology, a resurgent capitalism, and a focus on cosmetic issues that the 1980s ushered into the American consciousness.

In the above excerpt, Baraka lashes out at everything he thought stood in the way of liberation. It is ugly, nasty language. This is not a search for beauty in a traditional way. It is, perhaps, a way of seeking beauty by exorcising ugly: homophobia, anti-Semitism, racism, and sexism. Or perhaps it is a screed of frustration and rage. It may be all of that, but it is foremost a statement that delineates what he believed black poetry should be. And now, in the blush of the new century, more than forty years after that poem was written, our best and brightest literary poets would not necessarily embrace that idea of what black poetry could be. African American culture continues to add dimension to its reality, and many black poets are off in all sorts of directions.

It is a different story for the rap/poets. Many of the same issues and concerns that were voiced by the poets of the BAM were taken on by the rap/poets. In their poetry, one can see the same ugliness, frustration, anger, and dread. There was something in that poem by Baraka that didn't come from him but came straight up out of the asphalt. That was real. "Poems that wrestle cops into alleys / and take their weapons leaving them dead" seems prescient in the context of rap/poetry.

Gil Scott-Heron took us one step closer to rap when in 1970 he produced "The Revolution Will Not Be Televised."

> There will be no pictures of pigs shooting down
> Brothers in the instant replay.
> There will be no pictures of Young being
> Run out of Harlem on a rail with a brand new process
> There will be no slow motion or still life of
> Roy Wilkins strolling through Watts in a red, black and
> Green liberation jumpsuit that he had been saving
> For just the right occasion
> Green Acres, The Beverly Hillbillies, and
> Hooterville Junction will no longer be so damned relevant,
> And Women will not care if Dick finally gets down with
> Jane on Search for Tomorrow because black people
> will be in the street looking for a brighter day.
> The revolution will not be televised.

Here Scott-Heron presages the soon to become popular mixture of humor, "dissing" or insulting attitudes, oppositional resolve, and outright anger that rap/poets would employ. The significant thing about "The Revolution" is that it was set to a backdrop of music and was played on FM stations in black communities. This poem "signified" on the confusion that enveloped the black community at the time, relative to its collective identity. "The Revolution" at once criticizes the softening of the ardor of Black Power and issues a resurgent call to arms at the same time.

The use of music as a vehicle for poetic expression was not new in American or in African American culture. Langston Hughes had done it fifty years before Scott-Heron. Baraka produced an album of poetry backed by progressive jazz. Oscar Brown Jr. added his contribution with stories set to music. Nikki Giovanni used a mix of jazz and gospel. But it was the Last Poets who pushed this art to its next level. Their "Niggers Are Scared of Revolution" found its way into the heart of daily black life and opened up the possibility for poetry to have a wider impact on the construction of identities, realities, and the worldview of African Americans:

> Niggers are scared of revolution
> But niggers shouldn't be scared of revolution
> Because revolution is nothing but change
> And all niggers do is change
>
> Niggers come in from work and change into pimping clothes
> and hit the streets to make some quick change

Niggers change their hair from black to red to blond
and hope like hell their looks will change

Nigger kill other niggers
Just because one didn't receive the correct change

Niggers change from men to women, from women to men
Niggers change, change, change

You hear niggers say
Things are changing? Things are changing?
Yeah, things are changing
Niggers change into "Black" nigger things
Black nigger things that go through all kinds of changes
The change in the day that makes them rant and rave
Black Power! Black Power!
And the change that comes over them at night, as they sigh and moan:
White thighs, ooh, white thighs

Niggers always goin' through bullshit change
But when it comes for real change,
Niggers are scared of revolution

Gil Scott-Heron, the Last Poets, and many others, running on the fumes of the fading Black Power movement, created the conditions for what became the Big Bang explosion of rap that was soon to come. These conditions include the recognition that expression could change (oppose) existing circumstances, that there was a way to increase listenership/readership by superimposing poetry over familiar and funky beats, and lastly, that rap/poetry offered the possibility of a life of true opportunity.

NOTE

1. It's interesting to note that two of the leading poets of the Black Arts Movement, among many others, changed their names from their given "slave" names to African or African-inspired ones: Haki Madhubuti was formerly Don L. Lee, and Amiri Baraka was formerly Leroi Jones. So the taking on of "monikers" by contemporary poets of rap and hip hop isn't without precedent. Of course the blues tradition produced musicians who took on stage names but, in my way of looking at it, the blues men and women were not thinking about taking agency over their identity to the degree that the poets of the Black Arts Movement and rap/poetry were.

4

Defining Rap/Poetry

Who woulda thought; standin in this mirror bleachin my hair
with some peroxide, reachin for a t-shirt to wear
that I would catapult to the forefront of rap like this?
How could I predict my words would have an impact like this?

—Eminem

Rap, at its base, is poetry. We can find the poetry embedded and enveloped in a musical fusion of internal and external rhythms and melodies. The internal music emanates from the rappers themselves, through the organization of the words.

The science of this organization is found in the wider context of hip hop. As I said earlier, my sense of hip hop culture is that it is quite idealistic. Ethical. Multicultural. Inclusive. Competitive. Youth oriented. Essentially positive. But most importantly, no matter what phase of development of hip hop you examine, there has always been a sense of oppositionality at its core.

Consider the world before rap as viewed by poor inner-city young men. It was (and still is) a world in which success was measured by accumulation of material goods. Cars, houses, clothes, and opulent lifestyles were the accoutrements of the rich and happy white faces that cavorted nightly on the television. *Dynasty*, *Falcon Crest*, *The Love Boat*, and countless other comedies and dramas established the standards of the dream. And for most black men, there were only a limited number of ways to reach this wondrous life. One could aspire to succeed in sports or entertainment; one could advance in the thug life, outside the boundaries of established laws; or one could go to college, get a job, and rise up the corporate or public-sector ladder. But as Tricia Rose carefully and accurately points out in *Black Noise*, the impact of post-industrialization made formal entrance into the white world of commerce more of a pipe dream than a logical progression of an ambitious life for young black men.

So, when someone like DJ Kool Herc accidentally on purpose figured out a way to string cuts together to create fresh new beats that could be sustained to infinity, and somebody else, say Afrika Bambaataa, got the spirit and found words to fit Herc's grooves, a new world—the world of hip hop and a new way of expressing oneself—rap/poetry—was ushered into being.

From the beginning of rap (which is well documented in books like *Rap Attack 3*, *Black Noise*, *Hip Hop America*, and *Can't Stop Won't Stop* among many others), everything that existed in the world of the DJs and MCs, who played the beats and spoke the words, also existed in the expression. Everything was always there: both the playfulness and the angst. The joy and the complexity of urban street life were embedded already in the heart of this new literary art form. Indeed, mixed in between the taunts, party banter, and intercommunity information sharing, one could sense the rising anger and frustration.

In October 1979, the Sugarhill Gang produced "Rapper's Delight." They used music from the previous summer's smash hit "Good Times" by the popular R&B group Chic to spit out one of the first raps to be commercially successful. "Rapper's Delight"—one of the longest rap poems in existence, with eleven verses and over three hundred lines in its full form, lasting over fifteen minutes—was presented without pretense. The Sugarhill Gang had no apparent poetic aspirations. "Rapper's Delight" was what we classify in this book as a party rhyme (within the category "In the Tradition"), of which there are poems of quality. While this was a seminal moment in hip hop and rap history, this first commercial rap offering was rather—according to our standards of critique—unsophisticated (given where the art form would eventually go), hampered by a simple unvarying rhyme structure and an uncomplicated meaning.

But it did serve a purpose. It revealed the power and potential of rap music, and it revealed the inherent capacity of rap to contain more serious messages with more serious poetic intention. It wasn't long before other rappers began to use that same space, that territory that existed above the music, for attempts at real poetic expression. When Melle Mel, a member of Flash and the Furious Five, produced "The Message," the progression of African American poetry moved into a new era:

> Don't push me 'cause I'm close to the edge
> I'm trying not to lose my head.
> > It's like a jungle sometimes
> > It makes me wonder
> > How I keep from goin' under

I define rap/poetry as poetry that emanates from the cultural reality of hip hop. The consciousness that reverberates from hip hop's core creates the environment in which this poetry occurs. In other words, rap/poetry derives its definition from hip hop culture.

Hip hop, as a cultural reality following the Black Arts Movement, continued to adopt an oppositional stance toward everything and anything which reflected the world that dominated its proponents. Although hip hop was born from any number of cultural, social, and economic factors that were present at the time, underlying all of them was the existence of an instinctive and shrewd desire on the part of poor black and Latino boys to express themselves. And in so doing, they embarked on a deeper journey—namely to reorder a world in which they were unlikely to succeed—in such a way that their liabilities and vulnerabilities could be transformed into valuable commodities. Just as slaves once did when they put pen to paper, these first rappers began redefining everything.

Perhaps the most important idea embodied by the language of rap, and the language of African American literature in general, is that it can reflect an oppositional position. Words spoken can oppose existing ideas and supplant them with new ones. Perhaps even more significantly, rap/poets discovered that the speaker has the power. If the speaker then is given access to thousands of people who are lured by a magnetic beat, this power that comes from self-expression can be multiplied exponentially. Quite simply, this is, in my opinion, how Jay Z and Sean (P Diddy) Combs (as well as many others) have turned that personal power into wealth and influence.

The unexpected and unintended consequence of hip hop was that it tapped into a very wide segment of the world's population who felt (justifiably or not) precisely the same way. That is, the poor and voiceless peoples of the world felt powerless to express their frustrations, hopes, and desires in routine and regular ways. Rap changed that. Not all of these people were black, but they were drawn to hip hop by the power of the oppositional stance that rap took. It was attractive because rap spoke a kind of "perceived" truth and because the speakers were perceived as truth tellers. They were poets from the locus of the most intense disaffection. They were from the Bronx, Queens, Brooklyn, Philly, Bed-Stuy, Houston's 5th Ward, Compton. They were black. They were Puerto Rican.

What's more, by speaking in this new rap/poetic form, the speakers could suddenly claim agency. The transformative power of rap/poetry is quite amazing. To be a poet, to strive to tell the truth about one's life and circumstances, is also to take some responsibility and, consequently, some control over your social condition. This transformation is actually what coalesces into agency and personal power.[1]

And so, with an ever expanding base, hip hop grew and began to transform itself. It has earned the right to be called multicultural. This makes it even more difficult to characterize rap as an African American art form. But it is. While there are rap/poets all over the world, writing their poetry in multiple languages and from many different cultural perspectives, the form itself is African American. This makes, I believe, rap/poetry the first *literary* art form that African American culture has exported worldwide.

During the Black Arts Movement, the idea that someone would "use" a black art form wasn't surprising. The Jazz Age and the era of rock and roll had already provided ample proof that white artists were quite capable of appropriating black styles and sounds. Indeed, by the advent of the BAM, there was more than sufficient indication that black American culture informed and influenced American culture greatly, but this fact never seemed to receive proper acknowledgement from white artists or audiences. Artists as diverse as Buddy Rich, Elvis, Fabian, Buddy Holly, and Woody Herman, to name a few, had already scored commercial success by imitating black artists, so there was nothing new or surprising about the presence of MC Search or Eminem. But what is different is that these artists—as any other rap/poets anywhere in the world—*must* identify African American culture as the home of hip hop. Hip hop demands a kind of commitment to it or it will turn against you. Ask Vanilla Ice about that.

Still, what was possible in music seemed impossible on the page. For example, Stephen Henderson writes in his book *Understanding the New Black Poetry*, "if a non-Black writer elected to write on a 'Black theme' using a Black persona, and if he were as successful in absorbing Black expressive patterns as some musicians are, then indeed there would be real problems. As far as I know, there are no poems written by non-Blacks which have that degree of success."[2] Henderson was saying what most people believed, namely, "I can't imagine a white man successfully writing a poem from an authentic black point of view." Folks smirk, cast sidelong glances, and even Signif(y), comforted by the internal refrain: "You can imitate—Kenny G. or whoever—but you will never be as good as those you are emulating."

This is still largely true, but with the growth of rap, there are clear examples of rap/poets who are white and have achieved a kind of "absorption" (defined here as the capacity to effectively use saturation)[3] and thick description (a knowledge of a culture and its nuances) to the degree that they are capable of using this form and the hip hop "voice" in a completely authentic and legitimate way.

In *Black Noise*, Tricia Rose defines rap as "a black cultural expression that prioritizes black voices from the margins of urban America."[4] I would add that it privileges those who are not black with an honest and intimate exchange of cultural information about black people. By *honest*, I do not mean that it is always accurate. But Rose chose the words "prioritizes the black voice" wisely because when anyone raps, regardless of race or nationality, we hear that artist, but we also hear the phraseology, cadence, and rhythms of black America. We understand that that sound derives from black American culture. You can hear it in rap that comes from Korea, Germany, Palestine, Cuba, and France.[5] It is the sound of blackness. And in this sound is that very essence of oppositionality. Consequently, throughout the world, anyone tenuously connected to the dominant culture has found the form of rap/poetry useful in a full range of circumstances that, at their base, are oppositional. The history of struggle that accompanies the African American experience, perhaps even defines it, is sealed within the fabric of rap/poetry no matter where it occurs.

American rap/poets who are not black, such as Eminem and Big Zack, reveal uncanny absorption and demonstrate that the nature of contemporary African American urban existence is understandable. You don't have to be black to experience it. You might not (if you are white) be able to transcend the burden of your race, but you can definitely experience blackness in a deeply authentic way if your commitment to do so or your life circumstances require it.

As an artist, as an African American writer, this is not a bad thing. I love to see people wrestle with and try to deal with African American culture. I routinely ask my black American students—when they roll their eyes in resentment at a white classmate who has deep knowledge of hip hop—who would they rather this kid spend his time trying to figure out? Would they rather he be fixated on the complexity of KRS-One or Marilyn Manson? Common or Kid Rock? Would they rather young white students be aroused by the vapidity of neo-racist music or the dynamic and transformative quality of hip hop? I, for one, invite all who are lured by the intense expression of life that burns at hip hop's core to enter it enthusiastically.

At the same time, it must not be overlooked that there are good reasons for people to express concern and dismay over the infusion/intrusion of other cultures into hip hop. In music particularly, the dominant culture has historically appropriated what it wanted from African Americans and used it as if it originated on a movie lot in Hollywood. This type of appropriation has happened repeatedly throughout American history, particularly in the music and speech of black people. Music forms like jazz and the blues were routinely appropriated, first in a mimetic way, and then in more authentic ways by nonblack people. And like jazz in the realm of music, rap/poetry has become the first African American *literary* art form that has caught the interest of a global following.

Part of the work we are doing in this book stems from the need to specify the details of this art form that are culturally specific and which make it ideal, as a form for the use of others. In other words, when we choose to write haiku, we know we are using a literary form developed by the Japanese. Similarly, when artists choose to use rap/poetry as their mode of expression, they should know they are using a literary form developed by African Americans. The upcoming chapters explicate the characteristics of this contemporary black poetic form.

NOTES

1. In this pronouncement of the transformative power of rap/poets as artists who seek to know and say the truth, I am aware of the counterargument that discounts the purity of the rap/poetic endeavor. Some argue that record producers and the industry prevent rap/poets from achieving the loftier aspects of self-expression. But there have always been and will always be rap/poets who embrace and embody the highest literary aspirations. As long as this is true, the transformative power of rap/poetry will be present. Even if a particular rap/poet has sold out, there will be someone coming up who hasn't.

2. Stephen Henderson, *Understanding the New Black Poetry* (Morrow, 1973), 11, footnote.

3. For a full discussion of saturation, see chapter 6 of this book.

4. Tricia Rose, *Black Noise* (Wesleyan, 1994).

5. In this book, we have not included examples of rap/poetry from outside the United States, although there is much to consider and discuss about it. We plan an additional volume that examines international rap/poetry and its many forms.

5

Where You From? Local, Young, and Uncensored

Rap, for the first time, gave young black people fairly direct access to audiences of other black people. And for quite a while that access was largely unfettered by any censoring mechanism. Folks were writing poems about all manner of issues and saying what they wanted to say—how they wanted to say it—and no one was paying much attention. They could record their rap/poems, marry them to a beat on equipment they had access to, and then sell them on the avenue or give them away to friends at a party. Indeed, they could take their own poems, produced and finished on *their* equipment, and play the completed product at a house party the very next Saturday night.

It seemed to me that the generation, two generations removed from my own, had just been given freedom of speech. For real. When you review even the early old school work of poets like KRS-One ("My Philosophy," "Love's Gonna Getcha," "Beef"), Big Daddy Kane ("Long Live the Kane," "Word to the Mother (Land)"), Eric B. and Rakim ("Paid in Full," "I Know You Got Soul"), Tupac Shakur ("White Man'z World," "Dear Mama"), and Ice Cube ("Death Certificate," "Alive on Arrival," "A Bird in the Hand"), you can't help but be impressed at the honesty, clarity, passion, and instinctive ambition to compose poetry that worked on more than one level, that was indeed something more than lyric. That is, their rap/poetry was something more than the completion of the contract promised by the music of a song. It was apparent from the beginning that rap offered the creative writer a new vehicle in which to place a poem before it zoomed off into the great ether.

There are and have been brilliant rap/poets. Likewise, there have been and are many who are not. It is no different in that way from any other art form. Poets like Rakim, Mos Def, and Jean Grae must live and produce quality in the face of a blaring wind of mediocrity. Unfortunately, much of what is

31

offered on the surface of popular culture patronizes the expectations of that audience and is vastly inferior to the more sophisticated poetic expressions, which pulsate from just beneath the surface. Surprisingly, from that point just below the surface, moving downward, one is likely to be stunned by the beauty and power of poetic expression. Rap/poetry is a dense universe with layers and layers of meaning, sandwiched between braggadocio, vulnerability, and "blackismo."

It must also be said that rap/poets are mostly young, mostly unread, and certainly mostly nonliterary. They do not necessarily bring with them the pomp and distance of the traditional poet. So we cannot assume that they possess the conscious knowledge of poetic craft as taught to an expected population of poets. Young black boys, as much or more than any other group of marginalized and disenfranchised youth, are not prepared to be literary poets in the American canonical fashion. Yet, as you will see later, their command of significant literary devices and, in the best cases, their capacity to make relevant literary reference is often surprising.

But the age of the poet and the wide-ranging levels of quality of rap/poetry should not be reasons for dismissal. Consider this: if you take all the books published in a given year, there are precious few gems to be found in the piles. Even if you reviewed all of the volumes of poetry published by small presses, major presses, and university presses, very few would make their way into the public consciousness. In other words, when works of art are looked at as products, as they are in this society, a lot of crap is produced. It's true in fiction and true in rap/poetry.

But we don't normally establish qualitative standards of art by extrapolating the characteristics of the worst, and we don't normally define art forms based on unsuccessful manifestations of that art. *In the Heart of the Beat* hopes to contribute to the evolving discussion of a rap aesthetic. It offers some thinking toward an organized way of "reading" this work and provides an organized way of analyzing it by looking at the best rap/poems ever written.

* * *

Every rap/poem exists in at least two realities: that of the speaker and the listener. In rap, the speaker always forces the listener to enter his or her reality. In order to fully enjoy it, you (the listener or "reader") must accept the parameters that the speaker sets out for you. First and foremost, for reasons we will examine more closely later, you must remain curious about the language being used. The effective reader of rap/poetry must be open to a dynamic form of language usage that challenges easy comprehension.

The rap/poet is a traditionally nuanced, conflicted, clairvoyant, mad, eccentric, idiosyncratic being with the music of language flowing within. All that and more. In a society where public education, particularly for young black children, is woeful, it would be quite foolish to say that some systematic process is at work which yields knowledgeable and craft-conscious poets. Yet, through some cultural osmosis, mimeticism, and instinct, scores of young people have emerged using all of the traditional and nontraditional poetical conventions of the English language. And they do this with a smoothness that belies the deficiencies of the same educational development that I've spent so much time denigrating.

Perhaps more to the point, we shouldn't be prevented from appreciating good poems by the knowledge that the poet did not come by his or her skills through formal poetic training. It would seem that the nature of poetry demands that the craft and knowledge of poetic structures function in service to the essence of the poem, not the other way around. Whenever I have been confronted by a powerful poetic expression, neither my first nor second response is "Where did this poet learn how to do this?"

Rereading Henry Louis Gates Jr.'s *The Signifying Monkey*, I was reminded once again how young black children are taught to Signify. It is a capacity nurtured within the community. An African American kid on the streets or on the dirt roads who is incapable of Signifyin(g), or unable to recognize it when it's happening, is destined to be a victim. But as Gates points out, most black children are taught the intricacies of Signifyin(g) as a rite of passage. This instruction was historically conveyed largely through the retelling of the tales of the Signifying Monkey, which came in the form of poems, most often rhyming couplets.[1]

The hip, fast talk of the streets, with its sharp-edged double meanings, is poetic. And to survive in the urban environment, some intimate interaction with language is almost a necessity.

In some ways, it is the academy of letters that tries to build a barrier between everyday people and the art of poetry. The industry of poetic instruction demands competency before it will bestow the title of poet. But the truth, as evidenced in history, is that many successful poets of the past received little formal training. Walt Whitman, Maya Angelou, Emily Dickinson, and Jack Kerouac are just some of the often read poets with little or no formal education beyond high school. Even William Shakespeare never went beyond grammar school.[2]

It is true, of course, that most poets learned their craft by studying the work of other poets. Poetic form was certainly learned this way, and the eruption of new forms also sprang from the need to speak in ways different from the ways of other poets—all in an effort to differentiate, innovate, and discover better pathways to the truth. And as in any creative endeavor, artists will naturally construct and deconstruct form simply because they can. Sometimes these innovations are successful and lead to new forms, and other times they fail and disappear.

In rap, the process of establishing poetic knowledge has progressed in roughly the same way. Rap/poets study each other. They understand the history of poetic expression that preceded them and, if they are good, they work to elevate their expression, creating new sounds and new ways of speaking. This is one of the features of the dialogic qualities of rap/poetry. It speaks to multiple audiences and expects others to speak back. The history of rap/ poetry is marked by moments when various rap/poets have been locked in literary squabbles that have occasionally erupted into physical confrontations. I refer to these bouts of contention between rap/poets as literary squabbles precisely because they are in fact poetic combat and largely not physical confrontations. We see this in the "arguments" between Roxanne Shante and UTFO, Notorious B.I.G. and Tupac Shakur, Lil Kim and Foxxy Brown, and Nas and Jay Z.

Despite the sometimes dangerous consequences, there is a vibrant, often contentious discourse between rap/poets. This discourse is often focused on topics natural and organic to hip hop. And one of the significant features of the language of rap/poetry, as is the case with African American language in general, is the employment of Signifyin(g).

When I list the qualities of hip hop culture, you'll notice that the word "competitive" is among them. It is only in the last few years that I have come to understand how competition, perhaps a uniquely American way of interacting with art, has served to stimulate the growth and development of rap. My students have forcefully pointed out that without competition, particularly when experienced in "freestyle battles" between rap/poets (which happens almost every night somewhere in the world), much of the impetus for rap's growth would not exist. In this way, rap/poets challenge each other to grow, to be aware of the body of literature that precedes them, and to understand the structure of standards that will be applied to their work. And in this way, innovation occurs in rap/poetry.

Competition, however, can sometimes have a negative impact. When the popular face of rap suddenly turns insipid, small-minded, exploitative, and vapid, the competitive nature of the art produces more of the same. The airwaves are fairly clogged with clones of bad rap/poetry (sometimes with great beats).

The casual listening public is often shielded from quality rap. Most of the "published" rap/poems are never heard by large numbers of people. What is heard on mainstream media is heard because somebody *chose* to give it airtime. These "gatekeepers" have their own methods of determining quality. But rest assured that actual sales potential is at, or near, the top of their criteria. Although mainstream audiences are given the impression that the public face of rap is in fact its only reality, nothing could be further from the truth. Consequently, when the subject turns to issues of quality in rap/poetry, the most significant barrier we face is the notion that what we hear and see in the media offers a full description of the universe of rap. It doesn't.

NOTES

1. Henry Louis Gates Jr., *The Signifying Monkey: A Theory of African-American Literary Criticism* (Oxford University Press, 1989).

2. See J. R. LeMaster and Donald D. Kummings, eds., *Walt Whitman: An Encyclopedia* (Garland, 1998); Maya Angelou, *The Collected Autobiographies of Maya Angelou* (Random House, 2002); Jane Donahue Eberwein, ed., *An Emily Dickinson Encyclopedia* (Greenwood, 1998); Barry Miles, *Jack Kerouac, King of the Beats: A Portrait* (Henry Holt, 1998); and Park Honan, *Shakespeare: A Life* (Oxford University Press, 1998).

6

Toward a Critical Reading of Rap/Poetry

To listen effectively to rap is to be conscious of its literary components. It is to marvel at its artfulness when the poem is successful and to recognize and understand its weaknesses when it fails. To listen effectively to rap is, in fact, to "read" it.

As we wade through the ever growing library of rap/poetry, one question that continuously presents itself is: How much of this is the work of thoughtful poets who have struggled with the literary elements of their art to give us useful, significant, and effective poems that teach, inspire, empower, frighten, and challenge us the way traditional poetry aspires to do? In other words, how much did the poet know about and then use the parts of speech and elements of language to produce the poem we are dealing with? This is an important question because many people presume that the title of "poet" can only be bestowed on someone who produces intentionally.

It must be pointed out that one of the gifts of great poetry is the profound effect it can have on us. Sometimes that effect can turn on a word or an image. Take, for example, "the lesson of the falling leaves" by Lucille Clifton.

> the leaves believe
> such letting go is love
> such love is faith
> such grace is god
> i agree with the leaves

When I first read those lines, I was immediately touched. I think it was the ability of the poet to instantly seduce me into accepting the "faith" of leaves. "The leaves believe." It was the combination of those words and all that they

implied that made me so susceptible to this poem. And by susceptible, I mean
that I periodically return to this poem, and it continually offers satisfaction.
I feel the surrender and the naturalness of life within its lines. Of course the
leaves have no choice in the matter. When fall arrives, they must give themselves up. But Clifton chooses to see only beauty in that event. And in this
way she, at least for me, makes a case for hope instead of despair.

I use this poem as an example of how I can be surprised and how surprise
affects me. Rap/poets continually do the same thing. If you stop to pay attention, a hand is likely to jut out of the box and pull you in. You might see
the darkness of the urban night differently, or the sadness of a drugged-out
life, or the joy of possibility rendered new right in front of your eyes. That
is what rap/poetry is for me: a series of surprises. But to find them, we have
to employ some measure of discipline. Every rap/poem will not open itself
up for you. Every rap/poem will not reward your interest in it with meaning
or surprise. Every rap/poem isn't worth your time or energy. And some rap/
poems can harm you. So be hopeful and be aware.

Our process of analysis has three distinct stages. First, and most significantly, we must separate the poetry from the music. I realize the issues that
immediately present themselves when we do this. Some people, when they
first come into contact with this idea, feel absolutely sure that what they hear,
this amalgamation of voice, words, and music, is an inseparable combination. The beat (music), they argue, is essential, integral to any analysis of
rap. However, on closer reflection, it is possible to think differently about
it. As I've stated before, I reject the idea that you cannot separate the words
from the music. The words in rap are almost always more important than the
music.

Consider Jay Z's supposedly "final" production, *The Black Album*. The
poems collected on this disc vary widely in quality and impact, and the album
has been reproduced in various forms, with the same poems, essentially spoken the same way with different music. When DJs obtained recordings of Jay
Z's poems on the album without the music, a stream of "versions" of *The
Black Album* proliferated. There was *The Grey Album* (with poems spoken to
Beatles music) and *The Purple Album* (Prince music) and a host of others.[1]

Each iteration of *The Black Album* performs differently, and yet, the essence of the poems remains the same. On reflection, this series serves as basic
proof that the music that provides a home to the words is quite interchange-
able and thus less essential than many think. The interesting thing about this
series of productions is the way the words work in vastly different tropes. The
poetry actually takes on additional tasks. On *The Grey Album*, for example,
one cannot simply digest the words without reflection on The Beatles and

how Jay Z's way of looking at the world was so different from theirs. But this rumination is extracurricular to the actual meaning of the poems themselves.

Once the words are liberated from the sometimes overpowering influence of the beat and rendered back to paper where most rap/poetry begins, we enter the second stage of our analytical process. For this second stage, we have identified seven elements to form the basis of our analysis, as a way of "reading" this poetry. The elements of rap/poetry are:

1. Saturation
2. Language
3. Imagery
4. Texture
5. Meaning
6. Structure, form, and rhythm
7. Flow

These elements act as a guide to enhance our ability to interpret and appreciate the quality (or lack thereof) and effectiveness of rap/poems. Some of these elements, such as texture, language, and image, help us to understand issues of quality (as in artistic construction and execution). Other elements, like meaning, saturation, and structure, provide aid in our attempts to affix significance to a given rap/poem.

To make the analytical process interesting and to see what impact it would have on our discussions about specific rap/poems, I often ask my students to evaluate each rap/poem by ascribing a numerical rating system of 1 to 10 to the above categories. For example, we might take a poem like "For Women" by Talib Kweli and give it a rating of 9.646. The verses are as follows:

> I got off the 2 train in Brooklyn on my way to a session
> Said let me help this woman up the stairs before I get to steppin'
> We got in a conversation she said she a 107
> Just her presence was a blessing and her essence was a lesson
> She had her head wrapped
> And long dreads that peeked out the back
> Like antenna to help her get a sense of where she was at, imagine that
> Livin' a century, the strength of her memories
> Felt like an angel had been sent to me
> She lived from nigger to colored to negro to black
> To afro then african-american and right back to nigger
> You figure she'd be bitter in the twilight
> But she alright, cuz she done seen the circle of life yo
> Her skin was black like it was packed with melanin

Back in the days of slaves she packin' like Harriet Tubman
Her arms are long and she moves like song
Feet with corns, hand with calluses
But her heart is warm and her hair is wooly
And it attract a lot of energy even negative
She gotta dead that the head wrap is her remedy
Her back is strong and she far from a vagabond
This is the back of the masters' whip used to crack upon
Strong enough to take all the pain, that's been
Inflicted again and again and again and again and flipped
It to the love for her children nothing else matters
What do they call her? They call her aunt Sara.

Woman singing in the background

[Talib Kweli] (+ Background Vocals)
I know a girl with a name as beautiful as the rain
Her face is the same but she suffers an unusual pain
Seems she only deals with losers who be usin' them games
Chasin' the real brothers away like she confused in the brain
She tried to get it where she fit in
on that American Dream mission paid tuition
For the receipt to find out her history was missing and started flippin'
Seeing the world through very different eyes
People askin' her what she'll do when it comes time to chose sides
Yo, her skin is yellow, it's like her face is blond word is bond
And her hair is long and straight just like sleeping beauty
See, she truly feels like she belong in 2 worlds
And that she can't relate to other girls
Her father was rich and white still livin' with his wife
But he forced himself on her mother late one night
They call it rape that's right and now she take flight
Through life with hate and spite inside her mind
That keep her up to the break of light a lot of times
(I gotta find myself) (3X)
She had to remind herself
They called her Safronia the unwanted seed
Blood still blue in her vein and still red when she bleeds
(Don't, don't, don't hurt me again) (8X)

[Talib Kweli] (+ Background Vocals)
Teenage lovers sit on the stoops up in Harlem
Holdin' hands under the Apollo marquis dreamin' of stardom
Since they was born the streets is watchin' and schemin'
And now it got them generations facin' diseases
That don't kill you they just got problems

and complications that get you first
Yo, it's getting worse, when children hide the fact that they pregnant
Cuz they scared of giving birth
How will I feed this baby?
How will I survive, how will this baby shine?
Daddy dead from crack in '85, mommy dead from AIDS in '89
At 14 the baby hit the same streets they became her master
The children of the enslaved, they grow a little faster
They bodies become adult
While they keepin' the thoughts of a child her arrival
Into womanhood was hemmed up by her survival
Now she 25, barely grown out her own
Doin' whatever it takes strippin', workin' out on the block
Up on the phone, talkin' about
(my skin is tan like the front of your hand)
(And my hair . . .)
(Well my hair's alright whatever way I want to fix it,
it's alright its fine)
(But my hips, these sweet hips of mine invite you daddy)
(And when I fix my lips my mouth is like wine)
(Take a sip don't be shy, tonight I wanna be your lady)
(I ain't too good for your Mercedes, but first you got to pay me)
(You better quit with all the questions, sugar who's little girl am I)
(Why I'm yours if you got enough money to buy)
(You better stop with the compliments we running out of time,)
(You wanna talk whatever we could do that it's your dime)
(From Harlem's from where I came, don't worry about my name,)
(Up on one-two-five they call me sweet thang)

Scratches + Woman singing in the background

[Talib Kweli] (+ Background Vocals)
A daughter come up in Georgia, ripe and ready to plant seeds,
Left the plantation when she saw a sign even thought she can't read
It came from God and when life get hard she always speak to him,
She'd rather kill her babies than let the master get to 'em,
She on the run up north to get across that Mason-Dixon
In church she learned how to be patient and keep wishin',
The promise of eternal life after death for those that God bless
She swears the next baby she'll have will breathe a free breath
and get milk from a free breast,
And love being alive,
otherwise they'll have to give up being themselves to survive,
Being maids, cleaning ladies, maybe teachers or college graduates, nurses,
housewives, prostitutes, and drug addicts
Some will grow to be old women, some will die before they born,

They'll be mothers, and lovers who inspire and make songs,
(But me, my skin is brown and my manner is tough,)
(Like the love I give my babies when the rainbow's enuff,)
(I'll kill the first muthafucka that mess with me, I never bluff)
(I ain't got time to lie, my life has been much too rough,)
(Still running with barefeet, I ain't got nothin' but my soul,)
(Freedom is the ultimate goal,
life and death is small on the whole, in many ways)
(I'm awfully bitter these days
'cuz the only parents God gave me, they were slaves,)
(And it crippled me, I got the destiny of a casualty,)
(But I live through my babies and I change my reality)
(Maybe one day I'll ride back to Georgia on a train,)
(Folks 'round there call me Peaches, I guess that's my name.)

A poem like "For Women" would rank very high on our list of poems, as do most of the rap/poems we hope to include in a future anthology. My students gave this work the following scores: Saturation: 10, Language: 9.5, Imagery: 10, Meaning: 10, Texture: 10, Structure: virtuoso 8, and Flow: 10. What I can attest to is not the infallibility of such an evaluative system but rather how talking about the elements of a good rap/poem allows us to have more deliberate, intense discussions about an art form that demands just that. Consequently, the rap/poems included in this book do not have the numerical ratings attached to them. If you find such a process of interest, I encourage experimentation in this area, mainly as a mechanism to spur in-depth discussion about particular rap/poems.

Finally, because of the diversity of subject matter in rap/poetry and the general lack of acknowledgment regarding this diversity, we have made an attempt to identify and group these poems into ten thematic categories:

1. In the Tradition: battle rhymes, party rhymes, and poems of self-promotion
2. Crime and Punishment: poems about crimes and the perpetration and response to them
3. Social Critique: politics, race, culture, and social struggle
4. Inner-City Life: the urban struggle
5. Gender Discourse: issues of gender agency, power, and oppression
6. Relationships
7. Roots: neighborhood, family, and friends
8. On Hip Hop
9. Language, Satire, and Parody
10. Spirituality

The appendix to this book lists a number of examples in each thematic category. If our future anthology is published (as volume two of *In the Heart of the Beat*), the poems anthologized there will be organized along these themes; further description and examples of these categories will appear there.

NOTE

1. *The Black Album* remixes include Danger Mouse, *The Grey Album*; K12 of 12-N-Dirty Productions, *The Purple Album*; Jay-zeezer (Jay Z and Weezer), *The Black and Blue Album*; DJ N-Wee, *The Slack Album*; Cheap Cologne, *The Double Black Album*; DJ Cool Guy, *The Black Chamber*; DJ Zap, *The Blackprint*, and numerous others.

7

The Elements of Rap/Poetry

In the preceding chapter, we identified seven elements that form a way of "reading" rap/poetry: saturation, language, imagery, texture, meaning, structure/form/rhythm, and flow. Each of those elements is discussed more fully here.

SATURATION

When Stephen Henderson first used the term "saturation," he was making an attempt to measure the degree of "blackness" in a poem as a way of privileging the uniqueness of the African American poet. Henderson sought to value those black poets who had chosen to write from the black experience for black readers. He clearly believed that there was a profound distinction in the tone and tenor of the African American poetic voice that was immutable and perhaps beyond imitation.

Of course, the obvious problem that immediately arises when you use the concept of "saturation" in this way is that it leads to the ghettoization of black literature. And to a certain extent, "saturation" when used to denote "blackness" has fallen out of favor.[1] But I have resuscitated this idea of saturation in my analysis of rap/poetry in an effort to "de-race" rap/poetry. Rap is certainly a black art form, as I and others have clearly established. But this art form has proven to be exportable like the sestina or haiku. Rap/poetry is an art form that has grown past its racial boundaries. It is wholly adaptable to use in any racial or cultural reality. We do not want to forget its roots in African American culture, but we must also acknowledge its global usage.

Saturation is an important element of rap/poetic analysis. Because of this, I wanted to explore ways in which one might measure or at least consider the relationship of rap/poetry—no matter where we find it—to its history and cultural intention. I wanted to know how to evaluate a rap/poem's service to the culture that created it: namely, hip hop. The appropriation and redefinition of "saturation" seems like the ideal way to go about this. Henderson argued that to accurately understand black poetry, saturation had to be taken into account. In the same way, I argue that saturation might also be used to consider a rap/poem.

Saturation, then, is the degree to which a rap/poem, through its use of language, image, and ethos, communicates hip hop culture. Here one might insert one's own definition of hip hop culture. But for our purposes, hip hop culture is one that is politically oppositional to an imagined dominant majority (read white), overtly racialized (African American), overtly gendered, competitive, egalitarian, largely urban, and global (multicultural). Indeed, the application of saturation in this redefined way functions much better for hip hop than it did for the Black Arts Movement. One reason for this is that it is a more viable task to define hip hop than it is to define what it means to be black. Because saturation is a term of measurement, we will measure the degree to which one rap/poem embraces the ideas of hip hop relative to another.

One might best understand the idea of saturation as we use it here by first considering the following two stanzas. Both appeared to the public in the form of rap.

> This is game time
> My team is all hype
> Offense is fast, defense is tight
> The other team is nice but has no hype
> I throw my skates on and we can go all night
> Score the game point
> I'm the number one ace
> Drop my game face
> Meet up at our favorite place
> I get that quarter pounder
> With cheese burger for real
> The double fills up all
> after showing my skills
> The beef the cheese the pickles the bun
> After that I think its time for another one
> McDonald's. I'm lovin' it.

One might call this rap. It is certainly constructed in the poetic form of rap/ poetry. The line structure and rhythm of the words are clearly meant to mimic rap/poetry. But of course it is actually an advertisement, designed to interest its listeners in hamburgers. Now consider this excerpt from Ice Cube's "Alive on Arrival":

> Woke up in the back of a tray
> On my way, to MLK
> That's the county hospital jack
> Where niggaz die over a little scratch
> Still sittin in the trauma center
> In my back is where the bullet entered
> Yo nurse I'm gettin kind of warm
> Bitch still made me fill out the fuckin form

The difference between the two excerpts is dramatic. Some of that difference occurs in its level of saturation. That is, the construction that extols the virtues of a hamburger contains very little authentic connection to hip hop culture. Its intent is purely commercial, and it displays no sense of responsibility whatsoever to the culture it is trying to mimic. The writers of this rhyme couldn't care less about hip hop culture. It is purposefully exploitative.

"Alive on Arrival," by contrast, takes us deep into the inner city, perhaps on a Saturday night, and into the body of a gunshot victim. In this rap/poem is the harsh reality of many urban centers. Gang fights, gunshots, ambulances, emergency wards, and the wait. The account is immediately recognized by most inner-city residents: that sense of not knowing whether the needed care will get to you in a time of crisis—not because that care doesn't exist, but because nobody seems to actually care. Embedded in "Alive on Arrival" is a code of authenticity. It is clearly observed from the margins, and it is clearly oppositional, if not outright angry. This poem speaks from within the trope of hip hop.

<pre>
              0———5———10
McDonald's   ———————   Alive on Arrival
</pre>

These two examples can be placed on a scale. The first contains no saturation, while the second announces issues of race, class, and victimization in both direct and coded language. These announcements actually articulate its level of saturation. One way of considering saturation is to begin asking questions about a given poem. We offer these as a starting point:

1. Does this poem express an oppositional posture to the dominant culture?
2. Does this poem celebrate or glamorize the marginalized?
3. Does this poem reference African American ways of being (language, image, etc.)?
4. Does this poem and its speaker take agency (that is, does it locate the poet and the poet's community as the center of reality and profess truth)?
5. Is this poem politically conscious?
6. Is this poem gendered?
7. Is this poem racialized?
8. Does this poem suggest a desire for equality?

When one lays such a template of questions alongside the words of a given rap/poem, it becomes clear where, on this arbitrary scale of saturation, that poem resides. We can then say that one rap/poem is more heavily saturated than another. When we do this, we can begin to understand how some rap/poems are perceived by the public at large, by the media, and by the rap/poets themselves.

Rap/poets are definitely susceptible to trying to increase their public image of being "true" to hip hop by increasing the level of saturation in their work. Credibility and authenticity are lifeblood in hip hop and rap, and when someone, Vanilla Ice for example, poses as an authentic hip hop voice and is, on review, denounced as a fake, the result is devastating.

Rap is one of the few artistic arenas where class really matters. Rap/poets are expected to have been raised in the inner city. They are expected to know the streets, recognize both the beauty and oppression of urban black life, and understand gang and drug culture even if their poems are not about such things.

But saturation varies by degree—from poet to poet, and from poem to poem. As we might imagine, each rap/poet has his or her own political consciousness, his or her own moral and ethical value system. Saturation is also dependent on a poet's level of sophistication. The construction of a saturated rap/poem requires that the poet make use of language, image, and meaning to communicate his or her authenticity.

Consider the differences between Young MC's "Bust a Move":

> This here's a jam for all the fellas
> Tryin to do what those ladies tell us
> Get shot down cause ya over-zealous
> Play hard to get females get jealous
> Okay smarty go to a party
> Girls are scantily clad and showin body

A chick walks by you wish you could sex her
But you're standing on the wall like you was Poindexter
Next days function high class luncheon
Food they're serving, you're stone-cold munchin
Music comes on people start to dance
But then you ate so much you nearly split your pants
A girl starts walking guys start gawking
Sits down next to you and starts talking
Says she wants to dance cause she likes to groove
So come on fatso and just bust a move

and Public Enemy's "Can't Truss It":

But the hater taught hate
That's why we gang bangin'
Beware of the hand
When it's comin' from the left
I ain't trippin' just watch ya step
Can't truss it
An I judge everyone, one by the one
Look here come the judge
Watch it here he come now
I can only guess what's happ'nin'
Years ago he woulda been
The ship's captain
Gettin' me bruised on a cruise
What I got to lose, lost all contact
Got me layin' on my back
Rollin' in my own leftover
When I roll over, I roll over in somebody else's
90 Fuckin' days on a slave ship
Count 'em fallin' off 2, 3, 4 hun'ed at a time
Blood in the wood and it's mine
I'm chokin' on spit feelin' pain
Like my brain bein' chained
Still gotta give it what I got
But it's hot in the day, cold in the night
But I thrive to survive, I pray to god to stay alive
Attitude boils up inside
And that ain't it (think I'll every quit)
Still I pray to get my hands 'round
The neck of the man wit' the whip
3 months pass, they brand a label on my ass
To signify
Owned

Both of these poems are clearly saturated, but to what degree? Let us review them, looking first at "Bust a Move."

1. Does this poem express an oppositional posture to the dominant culture? *No.*
2. Does this poem celebrate or glamorize the marginalized? *Yes.*
3. Does this poem reference African American ways of being (language, image, etc.)? *Yes.*
4. Does this poem and its speaker take agency (that is, does it locate the poet and the poet's community as the center of reality and profess truth)? *Yes.*
5. Is this poem politically conscious? *No.*
6. Is this poem gendered? *Yes.*
7. Is this poem racialized? *No.*
8. Does this poem suggest a desire for equality? *No.*

Now to contrast "Can't Truss It":

1. Does this poem express an oppositional posture to the dominant culture? *Yes.*
2. Does this poem celebrate or glamorize the marginalized? *Yes.*
3. Does this poem reference African American ways of being (language, image, etc.)? *Yes.*
4. Does this poem and its speaker take agency (that is, does it locate the poet and the poet's community as the center of reality and profess truth)? *Yes.*
5. Is this poem politically conscious? *Yes.*
6. Is this poem gendered? *Yes.*
7. Is this poem racialized? *Yes.*
8. Does this poem suggest a desire for equality? *Yes.*

In the rap/poem by Public Enemy, the heightened political and racial awareness, along with its attempt to raise consciousness, indicates a much greater level of saturation than "Bust a Move." In this way, we come to understand the service "Can't Truss It" performs in the name of hip hop culture as distinguished from that of Young MC's. On the other hand, while "Bust a Move" might be less saturated than "Can't Truss It," it is important to point out that "Bust a Move" is significantly more saturated than the McDonald's advertisement.

It is also important to note that the value of saturation is relative to our need for it. Some consumers are unaware of the issues of authenticity and are therefore less concerned with a poem's level of saturation. But for my tastes, it is key. I want to know that the rap/poet understands and accepts his or her responsibility to hip hop culture.

Even though I've spent time and energy detailing the importance of saturation in rap/poetry, it unfortunately has relatively little to do with the quality of the poem. This may seem contradictory, but understanding a poem's level of saturation provides us with some measure of first deciding the validity and position of that poem within the universe of hip hop. Thus, the heavier the saturation, the more it commands my attention. The poems that most strongly serve hip hop are the poems that hold the most promise and beckon me to closer inspection. Yet, a rap/poem that is not heavily saturated, like "Bust a Move," can still be enjoyed. Saturation, in and of itself, does not indicate quality. Rap/poetry is more complicated than that.

LANGUAGE

"Every dialect is a way of thinking. . . . to speak is to exist absolutely for the other."

—Frantz Fanon, *Black Skin, White Masks*[2]

how many souls hip hop has affected
how many dead folks this art resurrected
how many nations this culture connected
who am I to judge one's perspective?

—Common, "The 6th Sense"

Borrowing Tricia Rose's definition of rap as "an artistic expression that prioritizes the Black voice,"[3] it becomes clear that to really understand rap you have to understand the references, the language, and by extension, the history of that language. Language and culture are so intertwined that if you are into hip hop, you are also naturally into black culture. However, just because the language of rap resides in black culture, it doesn't mean that Western classical poetic qualities are not present. To be sure, rap/poets confront the challenges of expression with the same devices and techniques all poets have at their disposal: metaphor, metonymy, synecdoche, alliteration, assonance, rhythm, and meaning. What differentiates the language of rap from the language of classical poetry, however, is that the actual words rap/poets use is very dynamic. The words they use are alive and are constantly morphing, triggered by popular television programs, characters, gangsters, mistakes, boasts, and bravado.

The words of rap/poetry sometimes exist for only brief periods of time. They transform in spelling, in sound, in definition. Indeed, the specific definition of words is more fluid than set. "Dope," for example, has many definitions, from idiot to cool. And the reality of all of those meanings can disappear at any moment. As a result, while they must be immediately learned and memorized, they cannot be expected to exist forever. Words in rap disappear. They simply drop out of usage. And if you don't know that or miss the moment when a certain word ceases to function in rap, you are marked by this ignorance. Indeed, for the rap/poet, by the time a word becomes commonly known (e.g., can be heard on a television situation comedy show), it is no longer useful to the rap/poet.

Much of what is said in rap/poetry comes in the form of indirect language or codes: words that stand for other words. This makes it very difficult for the occasional and casual listener to immediately comprehend the meaning of the rap/poem. People who merely dabble in hip hop culture almost always stumble over the language. Interestingly, though, rap/poets often provide a map, a carefully crafted space that signals to the reader or listener that the word exists differently from conventional usage. They fashion a way to say the word "game," for example, in such a way that you know they don't mean dodge ball. In order to fully break the code of a given rap/poem, you have to first understand the reality in which it came into being, and it is necessary to know *who* precisely is speaking. In "The 6th Sense," Common provides a good illustration:

> Some say I'm too deep
> I'm in too deep to sleep
> Thru me Muhammad will
> forever speak

or

> Under the Fubu is
> A guru

If we examine these lines, we can identify the function of coding in rap/poems. In the first line quoted above, the poet claims intellectual prowess and then claims that such intellectual intensity demands full attention. You can't "sleep" on him, and he's too busy thinking to sleep himself. In the second line, he claims Islam, in pre-9/11 reality, as a code for righteousness and black consciousness. Further code connects this religious reference to the Nation of Islam, the Black Muslims, who produce a newspaper (a mechanism for imparting "the truth") called *Muhammad Speaks*. All of this can be inferred from these two lines of code. And in this, we can reach past the words to discern a meaning, which might be something simple like: "You can trust me. I'm one of you. I'm serious, and I'm a political activist."

The line "Under the Fubu is a guru" is also wonderfully coded. To the uninitiated, casual listener who isn't conscious of the clothing designer and manufacturer, these words might seem complete gibberish. But if you know about the Fubu line of clothes, you understand that it represents black men taking control of the flow of goods and money in and out of the 'hood, that it is about black men capitalizing on the fashions of the inner city (instead of Tommy Hilfiger, for example). So "Under the Fubu" is a code that identifies the speaker as being about self-empowerment and self-determination, but also about not conforming to the norms of Western culture (ties and suits, for example).

Fubu represents one aspect of upscale inner-city life. But when Common follows up this image with "is a guru," the words become a statement of global agency. Common is saying you can't determine the intellectual and spiritual depth of a stranger walking by you based on the kind of clothes that person is wearing. In the line "Under the Fubu is a guru," he certifies and validates something other than the thug and gangster images that permeate rap. The language impresses, and at the same time, the service this poem does to hip hop is also apparent. In this brief excerpt we see both the effectiveness of the language and the power of saturation.

The codes of rap/poetry find their origin in African American literary history and in the nature of hip hop culture. As I said, they change quickly and always depend on the listener to have enough information to interpret them. The late great Big L's "Ebonics" provides a wonderful of example of coding and code translation at the same time:

> Check it, my weed smoke is my lye
> A ki of coke is a pie
> When I'm lifted, I'm high
> With new clothes on, I'm fly
> Cars is whips and sneakers is kicks
> Money is chips, movies is flicks
> Also, cribs is homes, jacks is pay phones
> Cocaine is nose candy, cigarettes is bones
> A radio is a box, a razor blade is an ox
> Fat diamonds is rocks and jakes is cop
> And if you got rubbed, you got stuck
> You got shot, you got bucked
> And if you got double-crossed, you got fucked
> Your bankroll is your poke, a choke hold is a yoke

A kite is a note, a con is a okey doke
And if you got punched that mean you got snuffed
To clean is to buff, a bull scare is a strong bluff
I know you like the way I'm freakin' it
I talk with slang and I'ma never stop speakin' it

Yo, yo
A burglary is a jook, a woof's a crook
Mobb Deep already explained the meanin' of shook
If you caught a felony, you caught an F
If you got killed, you got left
If you got the dragon, you got bad breath
If you 730, that mean you crazy
Hit me on the hip means page me
Angel dust is sherm, if you got AIDS, you got the germ
If a chick gave you a disease, then you got burned
Max mean to relax, guns and pistols is gats
Condoms is hats, critters is cracks
The food you eat is your grub
A victim's a mark
A sweat box is a small club, your tick is your heart
Your apartment is your pad
Your old man is your dad
The studio is the lab and heated is mad
I know you like the way I'm freakin' it
I talk with slang and I'ma never stop speakin' it

The iron horse is the train and champagne is bubbly
A deuce is a honey that's ugly
If your girl is fine, she's a dime
A suit is a fine, jewelry is shine
If you in love, that mean you blind
Genuine is real, a face card is a hundred dollar bill
A very hard, long stare is a grill
If you sneakin' to go see a girl, that mean you creepin'
Smilin' is cheesin', bleedin' is leakin'
Beggin is bummin, if you nuttin you comin
Takin' orders is sunnin', an ounce of coke is a onion
A hotel's a telly, a cell phone's a celly
Jealous is jelly, your food box is your belly
To guerrilla mean to use physical force
You took a L, you took a loss
To show off mean floss, uh
I know you like the way I'm freakin' it
I talk with slang and I'ma never stop speakin' it

Big L broke it down in that piece. At one point in time, the slang captured in "Ebonics" functioned also as code. Once the code is absorbed by the listener, it changes. It's one of the ways rap/poetry invents vitality. In one fell move, Big L demonstrated a facility with the language of hip hop and the inner city, provided instruction on its use, and depleted its power all at the same time. Anyone who attempted to use the same language in the same way was following Big L, which would have had significantly less impact than the original expression. Of course, Big L was simply repeating the language that was already in play on the street. But he innovated in at least two distinct ways: first, he introduced those words into the public consciousness, and second, he accumulated this slang and code into a useable dictionary, all within the context of a poetic structure.

Let's go back to Common's line "Under the Fubu is a guru." The implications of "Fubu" confirm its value as code, as does "guru." But something else is happening in a very subtle way. Common is "Signifyin(g)" that the listener might *actually be* someone who would pass by a black man wearing an oversized Fubu shirt and jeans and never even think that that man might be "deep" (read intellectual, spiritual). And Big L was Signifyin(g) that you needed his list of words and their definitions in order to understand anything else he writes.

Signifyin(g) is a major aspect of the function of language in rap/poetry. It is a way of saying things—funny things, hurtful things, confrontational things, lascivious things—usually in a purposeful attempt to ridicule, show affection for, or destroy someone and/or their reputation. All of which is usually done using misdirection, deflection, and indirect language.

Much has been written about Signifyin(g), beginning with the master work, *The Signifying Monkey* by Henry Louis Gates Jr. As Russell Potter writes in *Spectacular Vernaculars*:

> The historical and social significance of Signifyin(g) itself cannot be underestimated; it stands as the principal bridge between two kinds of distinctly African American stances: on the one hand, a reverential feeling for the past, a sense of ancestral voices; on the other, a deeply agonistic sense of social and verbal rivalry. Gates postulates two separate modes of Signifyin(g) corresponding with these two social functions: "motivated" Signifyin(g), which is parodic and agonistic, and "unmotivated" Signifyin(g), which is empathetic and reverential.
>
> Rap/poetry's language is propelled by the use of motivated Signifyin(g). In an art that is guided by the competitive energy of hip-hop, Signifyin(g) becomes even more valuable than it has been throughout the history of African American letters and discourse. The traditional reality of the poet in America, even among multicultural communities, has not been an openly competitive one. But with the advent of hip-hop, poets began to spontaneously compete with each other ("battling" as it's called) to demonstrate superior rhyming and Signifyin(g) skills.[4]

Metaphor, metonymy, synecdoche, simile, and hyperbole are the essential components in the arsenal of the rap/poet intent on effective Signifyin(g). Because the large measure of Signifyin(g) language is purposeful, the rap/poet must be prepared with a reservoir of effective metaphors and metonymous expressions. And when hyperbole is added to either formation, the effectiveness of the Signifyin(g) can be multiplied.

The Signifyin(g) and coding depend on the tone of their construction to render the final effect. The tone of a rap/poem conveys an attitude about the subject of the poem and the expected reader/listener. Like the manner of a person, the manner of a poem may be friendly or belligerent toward its reader, condescending or respectful. Tone may tell us how the speaker feels about himself, cocksure or humble. And we depend on the tone of the poem to help us determine whether it is confrontational, affectionate, hostile, earnest, playful, sentimental, or sarcastic.

* * *

According to Frantz Fanon, "to speak is to exist absolutely for the other." I agree. One's urge to speak is equaled by the need to be heard. But it is also true that it is to exist absolutely for oneself. When I think of the language of rap, I think about words that empower the speaker, words that identify, name, claim, and own the "I" in "I am." So when people become upset by what a rap/poem is saying, or how it says what it says, we must remember that the offending words and their meanings and images are, heaven forefend, a true and accurate representation of the speaker's world, of the language of urban America. The profanity, sexism, homophobia, violence, and immorality are merely reflections of the real or imagined realities of urban city (and more recently, rural) life.

It should be noted that the following subsections are an attempt to articulate the way I deal with profanity, sexism, misogyny, homophobia, and other negative aspects of rap/poetry's language. What we think about the treatment of these issues in a given rap/poem ought to be a part of the way we evaluate that poem's effectiveness. For the purposes of analysis, I have discussed rap/poems in this book that I would not necessarily have in my active library. For example, I think all objectifications of women, all gratuitous violent images, all use of homophobic language, and all outright racist statements, unless employed to interrogate their use and existence, work against a poem's quality and significance. It disappoints me when talented rap/poets reveal gross, unsophisticated, and offensive gaps in their intellectual capacity. And I strongly encourage listeners of rap to match their rap/poetry with their moral, ethical, and political sensibilities. There is so much rap out there, one need not compromise one's values for the experience. And so, the generally positive tone of *In the Heart of the Beat* is not meant to endorse the vapid, negative, and damaging aspects of some rap.

It is simply my feeling that the positive aspects of both hip hop culture and rap/poetry far outweigh the negatives, and when we turn our attention to any artistic aesthetic, it is necessary to articulate that aesthetic using its positive qualities as the normative expression of that art. Once we accomplish this, the antisocial and negative aspects are then put in their proper context.

It is true that rap/poets reflect the attitudes and beliefs they've been taught. Their families, their friends, the education system, and the media all contribute to a body of rap/poetry that takes sexism for granted, much as it does racism. In the best of the rap/poets there is a visible struggle with these attitudes and beliefs. There is a realization that their roles as poets demand that they examine their instinctive beliefs and reveal that process of examination to their "readers." But I encourage readers to formulate their own ideas and use them in the evaluation of their favorite rap/poems.

Profanity

One of the primary ways in which contemporary society tried to marginalize the power and significance of rap/poetry was to point to the use of profane, slang, and street language as proof that it (a) was not poetry and (b) was in fact merely inferior, scatological lyrics set to monotonous and repetitive beats. I can't help but think this is a version of what we thought about the Professor. Who knows what sense he was making? Maybe it was my immaturity, my unwillingness to accept his way of characterizing the world we lived in that made him seem so ridiculous. Who was I to say what made him free?

But when you step into the world of rap/poetry, digest the historical path that led to its creation, the language—the hard edge of this language—makes perfect sense. Putting critiques aside, profanity seems natural within the context of rap. It is natural because profanity has a known place in real life. Presidents curse, corporate executives curse, politicians curse, police curse, teachers and athletes curse. There is no profession where we won't find someone who uses words that are considered off color, profane, even offensive. Vice President Dick Cheney's curt "Go fuck yourself!" to a member of the U.S. Senate comes quickest to mind.

In most homes and in most classrooms, profanity is not condoned, not encouraged, and perhaps even punished. But as children, adolescents, and adults, we see the hypocrisy all around us. The mis-hit of a hammer that catches the thumb, a careening automobile coming at us, an annoying co-worker, and an ever increasing list of routine and extraordinary events cause expletives to take form. We curse. We might apologize for it. But it is likely we will do it again.

It is wrong, we are taught. Using profane language displays a lack of civility, of sophistication. Instead, it announces a coarse, crude, and inadequate understanding of the English language. Still, many of us can remember the rush of exhilaration we felt when the words "shit," "fuck," "goddamn," "motherfucker," "bastard," or "son-of-a-bitch," those words we were forbidden from uttering, were in fact uttered.

A part of the hypocrisy that our society teaches its children is that the consequences accrued to an adult for cursing are different (read less significant) than they are for children. But in youth, this is incompressible logic. Words are words. Early in life, most of us understand at least the rudimentary definition of most of the profane words we hear others say. And, perhaps more importantly, at an early age, we intuit how they are being used when we hear them used repeatedly. Few children over the age of eight (even among those who don't listen to rap) have not heard the word "motherfucker" enough to know many of its meanings and uses. The same can be said for words like "bitch," "shit," and "asshole."

Is it any wonder that when urban youth were given this amazing opportunity to speak to each other and to the world through a medium which had few demands beyond those which were already native/instinctive to inner-city dwellers, the poetry would contain all of the multipurposed profanity that swirled around them? It was natural—natural because the words were known and because saying those words was a direct challenge to their prohibition. It fit perfectly with the inherent oppositional purpose of rap. It went with the do-rags, the baggy pants, and the house slippers. It challenged the cultural imperative to maintain the hypocrisy of profanity as private language. Rap/poetry was intent on making the private public.

As a boy, living in north Philadelphia under my father's wing, I remember being impressed by the fact that I had never heard my father curse. I was probably twelve before that fateful day happened. He was trying to maneuver his '67 Cadillac out of the Philadelphia Zoo's parking lot and some guy almost hit him. My father looked out the window and called the guy a bastard. A bastard. That was the most profanity I ever heard come out of my father's mouth. And he was a truck driver. Perhaps he just had marvelous control when he was around his family. I don't know. But I did not grow up surrounded by people who used profanity all the time. So, in my work, profanity is used very purposefully. It is not natural to my voice, except in moments of anger or humor.

But to many in the world of hip hop, profanity is natural, an elemental component of their daily discourse. And how people talk will inevitably lead us to how they create art. So rap/poetry, within the context of its own aesthetic, is "normalized" profanity. And in normalizing it, rap/poetry built a wall of protection against unprepared critics. One of the primary objections to rap expressed by many of its middle-class critics is its profanity. Its loud profanity. Thus profanity itself is sufficient to keep many from listening to it. Indeed a certain comfort with profanity is nearly required to enter into the world of the rap/poet.

It is almost always true that people who don't like rap are quite likely to be incapable of quoting more than a line or two of some offending anthemic or iconic rap/poem like "Me So Horny," "Niggaz 4 Life," or "Bitch Betta Have My Money." They know just enough about rap/poetry to identify qualities that make it offensive.

But the rap/poet is unconcerned with issues of taste and preference when they don't emanate from the world that the poet writes about. As rap/poets know, their intended audience understands that the appropriate use of profanity is one of the ways rap/poets express their authenticity. And in so doing, the poets ensure a degree of freedom in their expression. Profanity serves as an effective barrier to interlopers.

Why should we let the threat and the actuality of profanity be the reason we ignore so much information and truth communicated in rap/poetry? I've been at high schools where I could not talk specifically about rap/poems that had some negative or immoral messages. I couldn't talk about them because I could not quote from them in school without the likelihood of offending some child or parent. And, invariably, at the end of the period, as the students filed past me, already cranking up their "pods" or Walkmans, I am always deflated to hear that particular rap/poem blaring from their headphones. What are we doing when we make it so that we can't talk to our children specifically about the words they listen to?

And why shouldn't we be able to brave up past the threat of profanity and obscenity to find out what lies on the other side? Once we are strong enough to step through the paper veil of profanity, there is much to see. Once profanity is not the point of resistance, our eyes may open to the yearnings, fears, joys, and anger that swirl in the hip hop world.

That N Word

I must say that my first reaction to the resurgent use of "nigga," "niggaz," and "nigger" was one of disgust. It triggered a rising sense of despair deep inside me. Had we come no further than that? Nigger is another word that I do not normally use. I can't think of the last time, outside of quoting a rap/poem, that I've used it. But I can't deny that in the private language among African

Americans, the word is in common use, replete with its multiple meanings, or as Henry Louis Gates Jr. might put it, its "ways of meaning." It is but another (along with homophobia, anti-Semitism, misogyny) of the symbolic ghosts that haunt the gates of rap/poetry. I now understand its function in rap/poetry, although I am still uncomfortable with it. The poetic value of those words is deceptive. On first blush, there is nothing in the word "nigger" (in all of its phonetic and slang forms) except the reflection of its speaker. At the first utterance, this word causes me to think its speaker is unconscious of its impact on the image of the speaker. When a person, white, black, or whatever, utters the word "nigger," I think less of that person, at least for a moment. My reaction is instinctive. A scar from my past.

As I said, it is momentary, for if the speaker continues on in an intelligent, interesting, engaging, or provocative way, the speaker's image can be easily rehabilitated in my eyes. But if the speaker has nothing more important to say than to speak in derogatives—unless that in itself is the purpose—I am likely to lose interest in what is being said. Consequently, in rap/poetry, the use of "nigger" must, for me, *mean* something. It must be an effective signifier of something other than a derogative term for black people.

And in rap/poetry, the word "nigger" often does serve multiple purposes. One important purpose is the attempt to redefine the word as a term of endearment and respect. Indeed, there are many who make a distinction between "nigga" and "niggaz" on the one hand and "nigger" on the other. They maintain that "nigga" and "niggaz" are benign forms of the pejorative and, in fact, connote affection. The rationale for this line of thinking is that these words are legitimate aspects of "street" language and ought to be recognized.

In Nas's poem "Memory Lane," the first two lines read: "I rap for listeners, blunt heads, fly ladies and prisoners / Hennessey holders and old school niggaz." Such a line might be received by most rap aficionados with a nod of the head in quiet understanding. Tupac Shakur could squeeze the word "nigga" out with the sweetest intention. And when a deft woman rap/poet uses it, the word "nigga" can draw blood. Rah Digga or Jean Grae or MC Lyte or Lil Kim—or any woman rap/poet—can code the word "nigga" from lover to rapist.

It is possible that the use of the word "nigger" in rap/poetry will lead to a time when it will be disarmed of its vile implications. But I doubt it. I favor rap/poems where the word "nigger" is not used. If it is used, I must be able to discern some purpose other than its apparent one. Still, on more occasions than I expected, I have excused a rap/poet for the use of the word "nigger" because its use felt right to me.

Gender Issues

Much of rap/poetry attempts to pervert and subvert the typical usage of profane and stigmatizing language, often in a brave but generally ineffective attempt to take possession of those words, as in the case of the use of the word "nigger." But once again, the language of poetry is absolutely reflective of the environment it emanates from. This is not excusing hurtful and demeaning language aimed at women in rap/poetry. Indeed, the presence of ideas, images, and language meant to objectify and oppress women ought to be a factor in evaluating the quality of a rap/poem. It is the job of the reader/listener to reject these poems if they are offended by them. It is the job of our educational system and the community (especially the family) to make these words, ideas, and images unacceptable both in concept and in reality.

I encourage people who are quick to demonize rap/poetry based on the level of misogyny and sexism that can be found in it to consider the reality and the lives of the rap/poets. Consider the landscape of their experience, the stories they've heard, the situations they've observed. The truth is, in the mainstream world, we know absolutely that, like profanity, sexism and misogyny are a problem; if we look at the statistics of violence perpetrated on women, it is clear that this country has a problem. This problem is exponentially multiplied in the way we raise our children. Evening television is filled with images of denigrated women. We tell ourselves that we want our children to be better than us, but we end up teaching them only what we know. And what we know has marginalized and abused women as a group.

The male rap/poet is caught up in a panoply of conflicting energies. He must authenticate his credentials by speaking the way he is expected to speak; he must represent. Through no fault of his own, that might mean (to him) that profanity—the use of the word "nigger" or "bitch" or "ho'" or a homophobic word like "faggot"—can be used as shortcut "codes" to verify his authenticity. This, of course, begs the question: "Authentic to whom?" And this line of thinking leads us back to life on the streets in America's urban areas. The male rap/poet often writes for men, and most of the negative images, ideas, and words used to the detriment of women are largely constructed for male consumption. As I've postulated, rap/poetry from its inception was a mechanism by which the private language of marginalized inner-city young men was transformed into a public one. This private language houses all of the misogynistic ideas that this society has privileged men to have and to discuss privately. When exposed in public, they are obviously horrific. In more direct words, many young urban men who write rap/poetry are unsophisticated in their understanding of contemporary gender political issues. Or they see those issues as false when applied in real life. They are taught to be sexist from birth, and consequently, when they attempt to explain their relationships with women or the behavior of women, they reveal their weaknesses.

In *Check It While I Wreck It*, Gwendolyn Pough writes, "Even as the Hip-Hop generation is vilified, alienated, and marginalized, certain elements within Hip-Hop work to vilify, alienate, and marginalize others. For example, while some rappers claim to be the new voice for the marginalized group of Black youth they claim to represent, they oppress and marginalize women and homosexuals. The rap lyrics that make constant references to "bitches" and "hos," "punks" and "faggots," work to create hostile environments for some women and homosexual participants in Hip-Hop culture."[5] Pough puts her finger on an aspect of the complicated discussion of the poetics of rap/poetry. Namely, how do we evaluate the complexity and power of rap/poetry, particularly its attempt to oppose the dominant mainstream, when a significant portion of those creating in this art form spend so much time vilifying and demonizing each other?

This seems to me a clear call for a discussion of aesthetics in rap/poetry. Some rap/poets do not fully comprehend the political weight and implication that may be embedded in their words. It is a question of sophistication. Some rap/poets have the capacity to oppose the dominant mainstream and also challenge the assumptions and presumptions they were taught as children. A rap/poet who is conscious of the political issues and concerns implied and explicitly addressed in their rap/poems and who has an interest in furthering the nature of hip hop will approach his or her art differently from one who is not conscious of or does not care about these issues. This, then, may be another way of considering the quality of a given rap/poem.

A number of male rap/poets are capable of expressing their feelings about and relationships with women in ways that open up surprising territory. Consider one of the earliest attempts at a love rap/poem, LL Cool J's "I Need Love":

> When I'm alone in my room sometimes I stare at the wall
> and in the back of my mind I hear my conscience call
> Telling me I need a girl who's as sweet as a dove
> for the first time in my life, I see I need love
> There I was giggling about the games
> that I had played with many hearts, and I'm not saying no names
> Then the thought occurred, tear drops made my eyes burn
> as I said to myself look what you've done to her
> I can feel it inside, I can't explain how it feels
> all I know is that I'll never dish another raw deal
> Playing make believe pretending that I'm true
> holding in my laugh as I say that I love you

Saying amor kissing you on the ear
whispering I love you and I'll always be here
Although I often reminisce I can't believe that I found
a desire for true love floating around
Inside my soul because my soul is cold
one half of me deserves to be this way till I'm old
But the other half needs affection and joy
and the warmth that is created by a girl and a boy
I need love
I need love

Romance sheer delight how sweet
I gotta find me a girl to make my life complete
You can scratch my back, we'll get cozy and huddle
I'll lay down my jacket so you can walk over a puddle
I'll give you a rose, pull out your chair before we eat
kiss you on the cheek and say ooh girl you're so sweet
It's deja vu whenever I'm with you
I could go on forever telling you what I do
But where you at you're neither here or there
I swear I can't find you anywhere
Damn sure you ain't in my closet, or under my rug
this love search is really making me bug
And if you know who you are why don't you make yourself seen
take the chance with my love and you'll find out what I mean
Fantasy's can run but they can't hide
and when I find you I'm gon' pour all my love inside
I need love
I need love

I wanna kiss you hold you never scold you just love you
suck on your neck, caress you and rub you
Grind moan and never be alone
if you're not standing next to me you're on the phone
Can't you hear it in my voice, I need love bad
I've got money but love's something I've never had
I need your ruby red lips sweet face and all
I love you more than a man who's 10 feet tall
I'd watch the sunrise in your eyes
we're so in love when we hug we become paralyzed
Our bodies explode in ecstasy unreal
you're as soft as a pillow and I'm as hard as steel
It's like a dream land, I can't lie I never been there
maybe this is an experience that me and you can share
Clean and unsoiled yet sweaty and wet

I swear to you this is something that I'll never forget
I need love
I need love

See what I mean I've changed I'm no longer
a play boy on the run I need something that's stronger
Friendship, trust honor respect admiration
this whole experience has been such a revelation
It's taught me love and how to be a real man
to always be considerate and do all I can
Protect you you're my lady and you mean so much
my body tingles all over from the slightest touch
Of your hand and understand I'll be frozen in time
till we meet face to face and you tell me you're mine
If I find you girl I swear I'll be a good man
I'm not gonna leave it in destiny's hands
I can't sit and wait for my princess to arrive
I gotta struggle and fight to keep my dream alive
I'll search the whole world for that special girl
when I finally find you watch our love unfurl
I need love
I need love

Girl, listen to me
When I be sittin in my room all alone, staring at the wall
fantasies, they go through my mind
And I've come to realize that I need true love
and if you wanna give it to me girl make yourself seen
I'll be waiting
I love you

The plaintive earnestness of the sentiments expressed in this rap/poem surprise us. We keep waiting for the rap/poet to change the language—to harden it—so that it conforms to our idea of the nature of rap/poetry. But this poem, to me, is one of the more honest of its kind. I believe LL in this piece. More importantly, it resembles feelings I've had. I know it is an attempt to get at the truth of existence and the desire to find love.

Common also succeeds with "The Light":

I never knew a luh, luh-luh, a love like this
Gotta be somethin for me to write this
Queen, I ain't seen you in a minute
Wrote this letter, and finally decide to send it
Signed sealed delivered for us to grow together

Love has no limit, let's spend it slow forever
I know your heart is weathered by what studs did to you
I ain't gon' assault em cause I probably did it too
Because of you, feelings I handle with care
Some niggaz recognize the light but they can't handle the glare
You know I ain't the type to walk around with matchin shirts
If relationship is effort I will match your work
I wanna be the one to make you happiest, it hurts you the most
They say the end is near, it's important that we close . .
. . to the most, high
Regardless of what happen on him let's rely

There are times when you'll need someone . .
I will be by your side.
There is a light, that shines,
special for you, and me.

Yo, yo, check it
It's important, we communicate
and tune the fate of this union, to the right pitch
I never call you my bitch or even my boo
There's so much in a name and so much more in you
Few understand the union of woman and man
And sex and a tingle is where they assume that it land
But that's fly by night for you and the sky I write
For in these cold Chi night's moon, you my light
If heaven had a height, you would be that tall
Ghetto to coffee shop, through you I see that all
Let's stick to understandin and we won't fall
For better or worse times, I hope to me you call
So I pray everyday more than anything
friends will stay as we begin to lay
this foundation for a family—love ain't simple
Why can't it be anything worth having you work at annually
Granted we known each other for some time
It don't take a whole day to recognize sunshine

There are times . . when you'll need someone . .
I will be by your side, oh darling
There is a light, that shines,
special for you, and me . .

Yeah . . yo, yo, check it
It's kinda fresh you listen to more than hip-hop

and I can catch you in the mix from beauty to thrift shop
Plus you ship hop when it's time to, thinkin you fresh
Suggestin beats I should rhyme to
At times when I'm lost I try to find you
You know to give me space when it's time to
My heart's dictionary defines you, it's love and happiness
Truthfully it's hard tryin to practice abstinence
The time we committed love it was real good
Had to be for me to arrive and it still feel good
I know the sex ain't gon' keep you, but as my equal
it's how I must treat you
As my reflection in light I'ma lead you
And whatever's right, I'ma feed you
Digga-da, digga-da, digga-da, digga-digga-da-da
Yo I tell you the rest when I see you, peace

There are times . . when you'll need someone . .
I will be by your side . .
There is a light, that shines,
special for you, and me . .

(I'll) take my chances . . before they pass . .
. . pass me by, oh darling . .
You need to look at the other side . .
You'll agree . .

Notice how in each of these poems, it is the vulnerability of the speaker that surprises and seduces us. The tools of surprise and seduction are in the words chosen. Common's line "My heart's dictionary defines you, it's love and happiness" and his extended metaphor of expressing love as a light are quite effective in lowering the shield of male bravado. Both of the above poems use carefully chosen words to express longing, desire, and love in a relative absence of gratuitous objectification or negative images. In "The Light," we are even provided with an admission of past bad behavior, which invites further empathy.

But as I said, it is often the rap/poems that are written by men for men that offend us. I'm reminded of a moment of surprise when I found myself at a dance club with a group of politically conscious women who were up for a night out after a performance they'd done at a local art house venue. AMG's "Bitch Betta Have My Money" suddenly blared through the speakers. I was stunned to see them, oblivious to the words that are not hard to discern, dancing and singing along to the chorus. And because the music that accompanies this poem is so compelling, it spurred the women to greater excitement.

In all of the volumes of misogynous rap/poems, "Bitch Betta Have My Money" is one of the most egregious. It is so offensive I've decided not to even excerpt it. Suffice it to say, this rap/poem contains all of the negative elements of a misogynist approach to language. It is unapologetic, arrogant, and full of juvenile braggadocio. Its language is abusive and assaulting to women. It is, without question, an ultimate locker-room boast fantasy that dehumanizes women. And yet the dance floor was full of men and women dancing as if it was an innocent party poem by the Fresh Prince. I was dismayed.

When men speak to men, it is bad enough. But when male rap/poets speak to women, it is perhaps even more disparaging. "Dear Mama" is often cited as one of Tupac Shakur's more effective poems. If it were the only poem written by him, our impression would be quite different from the one we might have after listening to "Wonder Why They Call U Bytch." In "Wonder Why They Call U Bytch," Shakur takes on the role of judge as he attempts to articulate the unfortunate qualities of a "bitch":

Look here Miss Thang
hate to salt your game
but you's a money hungry woman
and you need to change.

In tha locker room
all the homies do is laugh.
High five's cuz anotha nigga
played your ass.

It was said you were sleeezy
even easy
sleepin around for what
you need

See it's your thang
and you can shake it how you wanna.
Give it up free
or make your money on the corner.

But don't be bad and play the game
get mad and change.
Then you wonda why these muthafuckas
call you names.

Still lookin' for a way out
and that's OK

I can see you wanna stray
there's a way out.

Keep your mind on your money,
enroll in school.
And as the years pass by
you can show them fools.

But you ain't tryin' to hear me
cuz you're stuck,
you're headin' for the bathroom
'bout to get tossed up.

Still lookin' for a rich man
you dug a ditch,
got your legs up
tryin' to get rich.

I love you like a sista
but you need to switch
and that's why they called
U bitch, I betcha.

You leave your kids with your mama
cuz you're headin' for the club
in a skin tight miniskirt
lookin' for some love.

Got them legs wide open
while you're sittin' at the bar
Talkin' to some nigga
'bout his car.

I guess he said he
had a Lexxxus, what's next?
You headin' to his car for some sex

I pass by
can't hold back tears inside
cuz, lord knows
for years I tried.

And all the other people
on my block hate your guts
Then you wonda why they stare
and call you slut.

It's like your mind don't understand
you don't have to kill your
dreams plottin'
schemes on a man

Keep your head up, legs closed, eyes open
either a nigga wear a rubber or he die smokin'
I'm hearin' rumors so you need to switch
and niggas wouldn't call you bitch, I betcha.

I guess times gettin' hard
even harder for you
cuz, hey now, got a baby
on the way now

More money from the county
and thanks to the welfare
you're about to
get your hair done.

Got a dinner date
can't be late
trick or treat, sweet thang
got anotha trick to meet.

The way he did it
it was smooth
plottin' while he gamin' you
So baby, peep tha rules.

I shoulda seen it in the first case
the worst case
I shoulda never called you back
in the first place.

I remember back in high school
baby you was fast
straight sex
and barely move your ass.

But now things change
cuz you don't look the same
let the ghetto get the best of you
baby, that's a shame

Caught HIV and now you 'bout to be deceased
and finally be in peace.

So where your niggas at now
cuz everybody left
they stepped
and left you on your own

See I loved you like a sista
but you died too quick
And that's why we called U bitch, I betcha.

Dear Ms. Deloris Tucker
keep stressen me
fuckin' with a muthafucken mind
I figured you wanted to know
you know
why we call them hos bitches
and maybe this might help you understand
it ain't personal
strictly business baby
strictly business

So if you wonder why we call U bitch
You wonder why we call U bitch
If you wonder why we call U bitch
You wonder why we call U bitch

When male rap/poets speak to women, it is often similar to the theme of "Wonder Why They Call U Bytch"; that is, women who prey on men for material gain are reprimanded by the male speaker. The point of view and perspective, in keeping with the superiority of the speaker, almost always situate the male as arbiter of labels (bitch, ho), proper behavior, and appropriate interactions between men and women.[6] This is an awful lot of power to wield. At the moment a rap/poet's "voice" comes into focus, we must hope that that poet has also been appropriately nurtured in a way that his capacity to tell his story without dehumanizing women is up to the task. Of course, as it turns out, we are probably disappointed more than we should be.

One of the by-products of rap/poetry is often instruction. It provides a kind of educational tool. It teaches its reader/listeners how to talk, how to act, and how to be. When the meanings of rap/poems are positive and helpful, they are a wonderful tool. But when the meanings are negative and destructive, they can undermine parental, community, and legal attempts to encourage solid and uplifting life values like respect for women. This is actually a testament to rap/poetry's effectiveness as an artistic form. It does have an impact on its reader/listeners.

Thulani Davis, writing in the *Village Voice*, discusses a study of urban African American teens that indicated some of the damaging effects of "hip hop culture":

> The subjects of this study, then, have been raised during the rise of this influential culture and may reflect the long-term effects of the devastation of black communities following the civil rights and black-power movements.
>
> The most telling attitudinal change from the "movement" years is the absence of any influence of feminism and the open disdain for black women. As the authors put it, "Black females are valued by no one." The study's glossary includes six nouns used to describe males: dog, homeboy, playa, lame, sugar daddy, and payload, another word for sugar daddy. For women, there are at least 15, none good: block bender, woo-wop, flip-flop, skeezer, 'hood rat, 'ho, and trick all mean promiscuous female. In addition, there are freak, bitch, gold digger, hoochie mama, runner, flipper, shorty, and the more ambiguous wifey. Young women in the interviews also use some of these terms.
>
> In the survey of 2,000 teens, who were contacted through 80 community-based groups in nine urban areas, the "play or get played" ethos is equally influential among males and females, along with this disrespect for black women. The survey found that urban youth continue to engage in risky sexual behavior in relationships the teens themselves describe as lacking emotional intimacy and trust.[7]

It is clear that male privilege in all its manifestations is rife in rap/poetry. For some, it affirms notions of gender roles and the ultimate power of men. For others, it functions as instruction and indoctrination.

Given the dialogic nature of rap/poetry, it was only natural that as women rap/poets gained access, however limited, they would speak back to the men who dominated the library of rap/poetry. Women rap/poets generally write to reclaim aspects of their abused image, restate their power, and assert their voices. Eve's "My Bitches" is an example of a rap/poet attempting to reclaim the word "bitch":

> My bitches my bitches that'll change the locks
> My bitches my bitches that'll cut up your clothes
> My bitches my bitches that'll steal your stash
> My bitches are bold my bitches are cold
> My bitches my bitches that'll smuggle your drugs
> My bitches my bitches that'll hold you down
> My bitches even when you out of town
> My bitches is smooth my bitches is real

My bitches my bitches that take care of they kids
My bitches my bitches that you don't respect
My bitches my bitches that you always neglect
Yall niggas ain't real yall niggas ain't shit
My bitches my bitches let his ass go to jail
My bitches my bitches don't post none of his bail
My bitches my bitches teach him how that shit feel
Don't except his calls don't send him no mail
My bitches my bitches that'll fuck out your brain
My bitches my bitches that'll take the pain
My bitches my bitches that'll play the game
Ya'll niggas is weak ya'll niggas is lame
My bitches my bitches that'll stay in school
My bitches my bitches that can keep a job
My bitches my bitches that can raise the kids
My bitches are strong my bitches will live (echoes)

There is something in this anthemic poem that almost does what Eve set out to do. You cheer her bravado, confidence, and sense of identity. But the fact remains that like the word "nigger," which was used by whites to dehumanize black people, the word "bitch" is locked in its constructed meaning as a pejorative term for women. Still, Eve's attempt to work this word to her advantage helps this poem rise above mere profanity. It is a defense that attempts to use the language that was used against her.

Now consider CMG of Conscious Daughters' "Shitty Situation," which offers a different view of a relationship than Common's in "The Light." You might also see it as a response to Tupac Shakur's "Wonder Why They Call U Bytch":

Fuck, another day, another problem
A shitty situation that I'm facin, how to solve em?
You think it don't affect ya, but you should really listen though
To the conversation, cause the situation's critical
Let me tell you how it started when I first met him
Way back in the day at the Lake, and it was federal
Cause he was lookin good enough to kill a muthafucka
49 wasn't carin, yeah I'm starin, hell, I'm good to go
Said his name was John-John, livin on the Eastside
I said, "I'm CMG, where I live, and shit, I'm called by"
Did the little number-switchin, everything was fine
Jumped back in the Pont, dipped side and broke wide
See, it started off easy, talkin on the telephone
Most of it was drag, but I wasn't really trippin though
Thinkin about the sex, fuck the flowers and the love letters
That's the way it is when you're young and you don't know no better

Next thing you knew, about a week passed by
I was layin up in his house, and man, I couldn't keep quiet
He was diggin up in the guts like the muthafucka lost somethin
A Oakland Stroke with no joke, I mean, he kept it comin
Early next day I gave a friendly good-bye
A wet kiss and "I'ma call you" was his only reply
Feeling good than a muthafucka, shit, I can't lie
Lookin forward to the next time, the sex time was too fly
But plow on that shit, cause he never called
Never came to visit, never tried to get in touch at all
Never sent a message in a bottle or a telegram
Never got a page and I faded and I hate his muthafuckin ass

Now you ain't the one to play the trick
The one to get faded out of fade like the next bitch
So come Saturday, you can catch me at the Lake
Rollin deep in a Pont, lookin to set the matter straight
Then I seen his ass, just a little past Lakeshow
Hollered out his name, but he act like he didn't hear me though
Ran up quick, ready to send him to his grave
Kicked him, then I slapped him in his muthafuckin face
(Shit, you're out of your muthafuckin mind?)
So then I told him, "Yo, that's what you get for the disrespect"
The little bitch with him started riffin, but she didn't step
Back it on up, hoe, this matter don't concern ya
Just me and him, fuck around, and I'ma burn ya
She musta got wind of the fact that I don't play
Barkin up on that bitch-made nigga with the red face
But she didn't say shit, just stood frownin
But when I turned away, the sorry nigga start to clownin
That's when Jess hopped out with the glock 17
13 in the magazine, mean, nigga, don't spit
You better make like Hammer and start prayin
And listen to the words I'm sayin
I hate a shitty situation

Fuck it, one more uptug, one more hurl
In the toilet and it's peril for Daddy's little girl
Seems like a late night fuck got shit started
Cause now I got a baby on the way, and I can't afford it
But I ain't givin it up, no, fuck that
Cause it's a part of me, and ain't nobody destroyin that
Besides, I've been on my own, what—8 years?
Fuck a man, I be alright alone, just me and my kids
But now it's 12 months later and I'm mad as shit

Cause baby clothes and Similac and diapers is costin a grip
Plus I ain't had no sleep in quite a while
See, the late night fuck is now a late night hollerin child
Damn, I wish I woulda did shit differently
I wish I woulda got to know the man who was up in me
But now I guess I keep on keepin on, I just hope that you listen
To the words I speak, and don't have a situation

The dialog between male and female rap/poets is ongoing and sharp. The excerpts and complete rap/poems presented here demonstrate but in no way fully capture the combat that rages between the sexes in rap/poetry. What reaches the popular airwaves is largely one-sided, with too many male rap/poets preoccupied with words, stories, and images of the objectification and abuse of women. Because of the dominance in numbers and power of men, female rap/poets must continually use the language of rap/poetry to assert and reassert their identities. And, as Gwendolyn Pough points out, that language is already problematized by rap/poets who "vilify, alienate, and marginalize" women.

A young Queen Latifah, with her groundbreaking rap/poem "U.N.I.T.Y," tried to reorient the hip hop community with a strong response to the out-of-control negative representations of women:

Uh, U.N.I.T.Y., U.N.I.T.Y. that's a unity
U.N.I.T.Y., love a black man from infinity to infinity
(Who you calling a bitch?)
U.N.I.T.Y., U.N.I.T.Y. that's a unity (You gotta let him know)
(You go, come on here we go)
U.N.I.T.Y., Love a black woman from (You got to let him know)
infinity to infinity (You ain't a bitch or a ho)
U.N.I.T.Y., U.N.I.T.Y. that's a unity (You gotta let him know)
(You go, come on here we go)
U.N.I.T.Y., Love a black man from (You got to let him know)
infinity to infinity (You ain't a bitch or a ho)

Instinct leads me to another flow
Everytime I hear a brother call a girl a bitch or a ho
Trying to make a sister feel low
You know all of that gots to go
Now everybody knows there's exceptions to this rule
Now don't be getting mad, when we playing, it's cool
But don't you be calling out my name
I bring wrath to those who disrespect me like a dame
That's why I'm talking, one day I was walking down the block
I had my cutoff shorts on right cause it was crazy hot
I walked past these dudes when they passed me

One of 'em felt my booty, he was nasty
I turned around red, somebody was catching the wrath
Then the little one said (Yeah me bitch) and laughed
Since he was with his boys he tried to break fly
Huh, I punched him dead in his eye and said "Who you calling a bitch?"

(Here we go)
U.N.I.T.Y., U.N.I.T.Y. that's a unity (You gotta let him know)
(You go, come on here we go)
U.N.I.T.Y., Love a black woman from (You got to let him know)
infinity to infinity (You ain't a bitch or a ho)
(Here we go)
U.N.I.T.Y., U.N.I.T.Y. that's a unity (You gotta let him know)
(You go, come on here we go)
U.N.I.T.Y., Love a black man from (You got to let him know)
infinity to infinity (You ain't a bitch or a ho)

I hit the bottom, there ain't nowhere else to go but up
Bad days at work, give you an attitude then you were rough
And take it out on me but that's about enough
You put your hands on me again I'll put your ass in handcuffs
I guess I fell so deep in love I grew dependency
I was too blind to see just how it was affecting me
All I knew was you, you was all the man I had
And I was scared to let you go, even though you treated me bad
But I don't want my kids to see me getting beat down
By daddy smacking mommy all around
You say I'm nothing without ya, but I'm nothing with ya
A man don't really love you if he hits ya
This is my notice to the door, I'm not taking it no more
I'm not your personal whore, that's not what I'm here for
And nothing good gonna come to ya til you do right by me
Brother you wait and see (Who you calling a bitch?)

(Here we go)
U.N.I.T.Y., U.N.I.T.Y. that's a unity (You gotta let him know)
(You go, come on here we go)
U.N.I.T.Y., Love a black woman from (You got to let him know)
infinity to infinity (You ain't a bitch or a ho)
(Here we go)
U.N.I.T.Y., U.N.I.T.Y. that's a unity (You gotta let him know)
(You go, come on here we go)
U.N.I.T.Y., Love a black man from (You got to let him know)
infinity to infinity (You ain't a bitch or a ho)

What's going on in your mind is what I ask ya
But like Yo-Yo, you don't hear me though
You wear a rag around your head and you call yourself
a "Gangsta Bitch" now that you saw Apache's video
I saw you wilding, acting like a fool
I peeped you out the window jumping girls after school
But where did all of this come from?
A minute ago, you was a nerd and nobody ever heard of ya
Now you a wannabe . . . hard
You barely know your ABC's, please
There's plenty of people out there with triggers ready to pull it
Why you trying to jump in front of the bullet (Young lady)
Uh, and real bad girls are the silent type
Ain't none of this worth getting your face sliced
Cause that's what happened to your homegirl, right? Bucking with
nobody
She got to wear that for life (Who you calling a bitch?)

(Here we go)
U.N.I.T.Y., U.N.I.T.Y. that's a unity (You gotta let him know)
(You go, come on here we go)
U.N.I.T.Y., Love a black woman from (You got to let him know)
infinity to infinity (You ain't a bitch or a ho)
(Here we go)
U.N.I.T.Y., U.N.I.T.Y. that's a unity (You gotta let him know)
(You go, come on here we go)
U.N.I.T.Y., Love a black man from (You must let him know)
infinity to infinity (You ain't a bitch or a ho)

In this rap/poem, Queen Latifah deals specifically with the language that oppresses women and encourages women not to accept it. And in response, some women rap/poets have chosen to go beyond the simple attempt at reclaiming the right to self-definition that Eve does with "My Bitches" and go deeper into the male "thing." Jean Grae's "God's Gift" is an example.

"God's Gift" is a densely saturated poem written by a woman to graphically describe and display the sexism and misogyny women have to endure. Grae's poem functions on at least two levels: it articulates a strikingly complete bill of particulars concerning sexist behavior and, in so doing, demonstrates her understanding of the men who perpetrate it. She quite simply reverses the roles. She takes on the persona of her abuser. This may or may not be an effective way to strike back at sexist men, but it is certainly one way of attempting to (re)acquire one's agency. This is "God's Gift":

You can get mad
You knew the deal from the get go
If it's not you it's another bitch
It's all good
Whatever
Day to day
Bitch to bitch
That's how we live
Player, what?

I'm the reason ya'll breathe
The reason ya'll been here from conception
Reason ya'll believe in deception
And faithfulness
I'll make your destiny and fate twist
And when I stop comin around it's hatefulness
I paint bliss when you with me
Have you cryin you miss me
Lyin to you friends that you dissed me
I'm your world, kiss me and the globe turns
Sunrise and moon shine ocean tide shift in just the blink of an eye
Game transcends time when I spend with you
spit out incredible bull, lies are exceptional
Think you my prime-time whiz that I care about your kids
True is?
Don't give a fuck as long as you his
Hit it up until it's raw, no protection what for
I know you not shittin
Only call on me when you feelin forward
Only fuck top-notch bitches
Dime Pieces if they dirt broke or got riches
Single or rock bitches
I'm who you call your man
Who you call your fam
Who you call late night in a jam
4:30 am bawlin to me, I'm just plain ballin you see
being with one bitch is boring to me
I say variety is the fruit of life
it's not my fault that every woman is the foolish type
and after me you cop an attitude like you's a dyke
you fell for it let the dick call it
Killin it like

See this style
didn't even use game to get you

you know you been open wide off me since the day I met you
never let go of me
when we fuckin you love me
when we in the streets you motherfuckin bitches touch me
I think it's funny you call me your honey
I call you when I'm feeling horny
you say when I'm not around your pussy feelin lonely
I told you never let a bitch own me
still you buy me shit
Iceburg, Sony, Hitachi, a Motorola, Dreamcast, and four controllers
trip to Atlantic City like we some high rollers
think you gonna lock it down
even write me letters every time you outta town
don't even read em
what the fuck I need a wife for
I lead the life of a free man
told you I was a player since the first hand was dealt
want me to meet your family?
Well, I got some news for them
If you got sisters
Put the move on them
Let loose two on em
Loose screw on em
Mom's too, even better get up than you
And your dad know the deal
He's a nigga
I'm saying the older you get the better you get at playin for real

I've had em all from the whores to good girls galore
Twins to wheelchair bitches
Freaks to married girls turned frigid
Classy models to pigeons
You not special cause you went and cross your feelings on another level
Another day another hustle
You no different
I'm not the daddy for your children
Tell me you're separated, divorce pending
Listen the only position you fill
is pussy you're in
I never spend a dime on you
My time's precious
You whining on the jack about lack of respect for women
What if my daughter was to grow up and meet a villain like me
Fuck it I ain't got no children
If I did I'd teach them better than you've been

Your self-esteem is all fucked
Musta been busted when growin up
Cause pretty bitches know enough
Now you're mad blowin up
Whatever listen,
I gotta bounce
Your best friend's on the way to my house

This poem challenges the power structure; it demonstrates how Grae tries to "speak" back at and against male sexism. It is an effort that is harrowing to say the least. But I find myself asking, "Is the level of degradation she must subject herself to in order to tell us this truth worth it?" She must participate in the dehumanizing language that men use to degrade women in order to make her point and to demonstrate her understanding of the male psyche. In the end, for me, it is worth it. I think it is a successful foray in an unpleasant reality that reveals important information. We end up knowing that the predator she has portrayed is an accurate representation of some of the men young women must routinely defend themselves against.

It is true that rap/poets reflect the attitudes and beliefs they've been taught. Among the strongest rap/poets, there is a realization that their roles as poets demand that they examine their instinctive beliefs and reveal that process of examination to their readers. The idea of a respectful equality among genders, I believe, is inscribed in the definition of hip hop. Unfortunately, it is not often seen in the popular manifestation of hip hop culture. Hip hop suffers to some degree from an inability to live up to its potential. Sexism continues to be an obvious problem in rap/poetry as it is in hip hop.

And sexism, like racism, has a real, visceral impact. It is sadly true that the involvement and significance of women in the development of hip hop culture has been marginalized. The truth is that women have been active at all stages of the evolution of hip hop culture from its inception, which is why gender equality is explicit and organic in an idealized definition of hip hop. Scores of relatively unknown women rap/poets create and produce just out of the public eyesight.[8] In this regard, there are two points to be made. The involvement of talented, strong, and effective women throughout the evolution of hip hop has had an impact in many discernible ways. But this has not, by and large, had an improving effect on the degree to which sexism and misogyny remain a problem.

Unfortunately, not enough people who might be able to engage in more enlightened discussion with young people about the sexism and misogyny in rap/poetry know the body of rap/poetry well enough to do so. When it comes to the language and the significance of that language in rap/poetry, the absence of influence—caused by a lack of knowledge about rap/poetry and its implications—of the black middle class, in particular, exacerbates the problem of morality and values. The targeted reader/listeners of rap/poetry are left with little or no guidance other than their peers.

Finally, when it comes to evaluating rap/poetry, we must consider the language used to activate the other elements. Words hold everything together. Without words there are no poems. But how well does the rap/poet relate to words? Does the rap/poet make clever use of the parts of speech? How interesting and complex are the codes used and what is their purpose in a particular poem? I usually can't help but evaluate how ambitious (or lazy) the rap/poet seems to be in word selection.

It gets trickier when it comes to gender issues. I am especially sensitive to language that dehumanizes or objectifies women. When it is conscious, deliberate, gratuitous, and damaging, as in "Bitch Betta Have My Money" for example, I might eliminate that piece from my active library. But a certain percentage of the rap/poems that are sexist are unconsciously so and force me to make even finer distinctions. Still, if I were to put a negative value on abusive, sexist language, it would be high. Said another way, if a rap/poem feels uncomfortable to me when it tries to portray or address women, I usually rate it as inferior to other rap/poems that don't make me feel that way. As a check on my own consciousness, I often ask myself, "Would I feel comfortable listening to this rap/poem if a woman was sitting beside me?" If the answer is "no," I will usually eliminate that poem from my listening library.

It also makes a difference to me if the rap/poem uses homophobic language that is aimed specifically at denigrating gays, lesbians, or other nonheteronormative people. It is likely that I could never accept that rap/poem as being "effective" or "good." There is so much rap/poetry from which to choose that eliminating poems that don't stand up to our highest standards doesn't significantly diminish our ability to enjoy rap and participate in the discussions that are going on among these hip hop griots.

In summary, when we consider the quality and effectiveness of language in a given rap/poem, I would suggest a process that encourages a listener/reader to:

- Identify metaphors and similes; evaluate the quality, diversity, and complexity of their construction.
- Identify other elements of speech employed, particularly alliteration, assonance, metonymy, synecdoche, personification, and onomatopoeia. Consider how effectively the poet has made use of these techniques to render the language of the rap/poem interesting and successful.

Also, ask the following questions:

- What is the tone of this poem? Is the tone appropriate to the subject of the rap/poem?
- Does the rap/poet use any form of Signifyin(g)? Does the rap/poet seem conscious of the power and capacity of Signifyin(g)?
- Does the rap/poet use language as a manifestation of agency? That is, is the poet in command of the language of the piece?
- Is some degree of surprise embedded in the words of this poem?
- Does the rap/poet seem to have a wide vocabulary from which to choose the words that express most accurately her or his point of view?
- Can you point to a specific line in which the rap/poet used precisely the right word at precisely the right time?
- Is there a sense of originality in the language used by the rap/poet?

IMAGERY

Unlike saturation, the quality of the images presented in a rap/poem gets us much closer to a discussion of its quality. Successful rap/poems engage us in the same way all poetry does. Concepts and emotions are often transformed into pictures constructed from words. The employment of sensory perception—whether or not the poet uses all of her or his senses of sight, smell, taste, sound, and touch to bring us into the body of the experience of the poem—is crucial to how we gauge a rap/poem's quality. In the end, we feel connected to the sentiment and perhaps even the action or emotions expressed when a rap/poet engages all our senses.

We pay particular attention to these images when they are concrete and specific. When Common says, "If heaven had a height / you would be that tall," the image of a towering presence is struck. Or consider this from Plug 2 from De La Soul's "I Am I Be": "I choose to run from the rays of the burning sun / and dodge a needle washing up upon a sandy shore," or this from Tupac Shakur's "Dear Mama":

> And I could see you comin home after work late
> You're in the kitchen tryin to fix us a hot plate
> Ya just workin with the scraps you was given
> And mama made miracles every Thanksgivin

Images are full of their own magic. When they are carefully and interestingly constructed, they surprise and enchant us. On its own, a well-crafted image is capable of forcing us into reflection and melancholy. We grab on to the concreteness of the image and slip into the dream of the scene being described. Indeed, most rap poems, especially the most effective, attempt to tell a story. In this context, story is simply an accumulation of images, which fit together as a whole.

This is not meant to imply that the constructed images rap/poets create conform to some classical hierarchy of significance. Indeed, if there is a hierarchy of images, it serves to reorder the dominant perception of "good" and "normal." Beauty can shine through in the bleakest of environments. Jean Grae, one of the most effective rap/poets, has the capacity to take us to the depths of despair. And yet, there remains beauty at the core of her constructed images. Even when she talks about suicide in "Take Me," she does so in such a vivid way that the objects in this poem fairly radiate. It is sadly magnetic, beautiful. The best of the rap/poets provide images that envelope readers/listeners in a recognizable reality, full of meanings and truths. Here is an excerpt from "Take Me":

> You see this dirty knife on the floor, this chrome nine in my hand
> These foul thoughts in my conscious, constantly understand
> See we taught to believe if you can touch it and see it, it must
> Be real so go believe it. But I've never seen Jesus
> I've never seen God, so he's only a thesis
> And I'm questioning all these things in my time to depart
> I know it's written, suicide is giving hell and devils privilege
> Only wicked heathens commit it, sin of ages, well fuck it, bring it!
> Lately I've been waking early mornings screaming
> "Save me," dreams of seven horsemen chasing Jean, hastening speed
> So I'm raising the barrel envisioning marrow
> Splashed on the wall and polka dotting all my apparel
> And maybe, Ginsu blades through skin will slay
> And split thin veins instead of loading clips that spray
> And if I'm meant to stay, then I'll just pass through the gates
> And fall a long way back to Earth, so why don't you just
>
> (Take Me) Through the shadows of valley of death, God
> (Take me) when I'm shooting, taking last breaths hard
> (Baby) I want to walk through the valleys praying lord
> Will you help me, save me God, won't you tell me, tell me
> (Take me) 'Cause I'm losing my faith, bless me
> (Take me) 'Cause this world just want to test me
>
> You can see the pain twist my face from a distance
> The body's windows glistening red hot from all of the indo
> Thinking of my next of kinfolk, my mama
> Opening doors, crimson billows spread out on the pillows and floor
> I gotta block it out. I'm set on knocking out

> Lock and aim and I'm dropping my frame quick when I pop in the brain
> And if God's omnipotent, will he slip in and change
> And move the pistol so it shoots out of range and the lead whistles
> (Baby) Maybe he's just playing it'll ricochet and cripple me
> Strictly for questioning, give me life to the pain
> Sickle shaped body bent in the middle, so little
> Kids who pass me harass me and giggle. My figure's
> Itching to touch on the answers. Hard headed like
> Exotic dancers' nipples, picturing the bullets ripping the skin
> On the mantle I'm holding, pull back and blow the wick
> Right off the candle, throw a kiss and told the world how to focus
> So now (take me . . . take me)

There is a beauty in the symmetry of the images Grae conjures. We are there with her. In many ways, the images of the rap/poet are diametrically opposed to the exalted images of traditional poetry. Indeed, second only to language, imagery is one of the methods rap/poets use to confront the status quo. They challenge our ideas about what is. Do you really want to know what it's like to live in Houston's 5th Ward? Do you really want to experience a gang bang? Be shot? To shoot someone? Would you really like to see the worst city block in the worst part of a bad city? The Platonic notion of the poet's concern for beauty must be reconstructed for this journey. And it begins first with the pictures.

As Tricia Rose makes clear, rap has historically been local.[9] Its focus is generally limited to specific geographic dimensions. A neighborhood. A street. A clique. And because rap/poetry reflects the reality of the people and their dreams from which the poet emerged, the images the poets create must be accurate. While the images of a crack dealer embraced by the shadows of a darkened city street or that same dealer being gunned down thirty seconds later might be unpleasant, to the poet those images might be real or imagined realities that must be expressed, reported. To not do so would seem inauthentic to the poet's intended audience.

Of course, this symbiotic relationship between the poet and the poet's audience is easily perverted when poets are "encouraged" by record companies to purposefully "authenticate" their work through images the community expects even when instinct might be pushing the poets in newer, more complicated directions. This is an important consideration. However, we must trust the poet to provide us with accurate images of our own existence. The image is where we enter the story of the poem.

Rap/poets generate at least two types of images: (1) simple images composed of sensory components such as color, shape, smell, sound, and taste, and (2) complex images that provide the details of the simple image but are augmented with information that adds richness and dimension to that image. Metaphor and simile are essential tools in complicating a simple image. Metaphor and simile add qualitative information to the concrete and specific descriptions that form an image.

In "A Million Eyes," Apani paints an excruciatingly horrible picture of a rape and, at the same time, makes a comparison of this violence to lynching. Metaphor and simile enrich the following excerpt:

> I stood up to be counted
> You beat me down
> Surrounded by a million eyes
> My bones crackin' sounded like Hell's thunder
> Under attack arms pinned back
> Blurry vision, bloody
> Couldn't see who first stuck me
> Between my thighs—I felt ugly
> They took turns to fuck me
> Beneath southern skies
> They wanna shame me
> Make me think I'm nothing
> But I'm still every woman, plus
> Won't give 'em the satisfaction—of reaction
> These bastards—will have to kill me
> Spill my blood on the roots of this willow tree
> Where strange fruit swings from the limbs a plenty
> If that be G-d's will, then so it is
> I'd rather die than birth and raise his kids
> I'll leave this black hole with my soul intact
> Never look back not once
> [If] He put his tongue in my mouth
> I'ma spit on his fronts
> Never give in
> Gotta go out scrapping
> Even if I can't win (what)

The images constructed in "A Million Eyes" are stunning, singular, and the mark of a confident poet. They flow together to form a scene that lives in our mind. I was particularly moved by the lines "blurry vision, bloody, can't see who first stuck me / between my thighs, I felt ugly / they took turns to fuck me." The surprise and power that result from this complex image are overpowering. We see this woman lying there, being assaulted, and we hear her resolve, her defiance. Our empathy is foregone. Furthermore, this image of rape is made more complicated when the poet alludes to the lynching of black men: "Spill my blood on the roots of this willow tree / Where strange fruit swings from the limbs a plenty." The blood from black men that used to drip down the branches of this southern tree is now replaced by the blood of this black woman. Recalling this particular history at this moment works to bring the physical violation of black women on par with the physical violation of black men. The rape of black women is just as horrific and devastating as the lynching of black men. This is indeed a complex image Apani weaves.

In "Juicy," Notorious B.I.G.'s classic rap/poem, the metaphor is buried beneath the images. The images in the following excerpt appear on first glance to be quite simple. Indeed, the poet employs the use of lists to give life to them. But it's the list itself that becomes metaphor and transports us back in time:

> It was all a dream,
> I used to read Word Up magazine:
> Salt 'n'Pepa and Heavy D up in the limousine.
> Hanging pictures on my wall,
> Every Saturday, Rap Attack, Mr. Magic, Marley Marl.
> I let my tape rock 'til my tape popped,
> Smokin' weed in Bambu, sippin' on private stock.
> Way back, when I had the red and black lumberjack
> With the hat to match.
> Remember Rappin' Duke? (Duh-ha, duh-ha)
> You never thought that hip hop would take it this far.
> Now I'm in the limelight cuz I rhyme tight
> Time to get paid, blow up like the World Trade.
> A born sinner, the opposite of a winner.
> Remember when I used to eat sardines for dinner?

We are treated to all manner of images in this piece. It was, in fact, one of Notorious B.I.G.'s strongest qualities as a poet. He was quite skilled in the creation of both simple and complex images. In the first stanza, we imagine the rap/poet lying on the bed, listening to the radio, reading a magazine. But that stanza is made powerful by its series of complex images. *Word Up* magazine is a dense image all unto itself. It speaks of a specific time in the evolution of rap. One who is familiar with its brief influence can imagine the cover, any cover, with its dark, rich hues through which shards of yellow peaked. The face of Run DMC or some other rapper peered out at you. And Notorious B.I.G. lets us know it was him reading the magazine. And you can see it. A young, heavy-set black man studying his mentors, seeing Salt-N-Pepa and Heavy D putting on airs. We can feel the anticipation, the hunger in the first line. We can see this same young poet marking his wall with pictures of his heroes. And finally there is the image of Biggie lying on the bed, listening to the brothers who would ultimately influence him.

Or, for another example, take the old-school rap/poem "The Message," attributed to Melle Mel:

> Broken glass everywhere
> People pissin' on the stairs, you know they just don't care
> I can't take the smell, can't take the noise
> Got no money to move out, I guess I got no choice
> Rats in the front room, roaches in the back
> Junkies in the alley with a baseball bat
> I tried to get away but I couldn't get far
> 'cuz a man with a tow truck repossessed my car

At work is a heavily saturated series of images that convey complex forces. This description combines common ghetto images with the despair and irony of immobility. Once you've described such a scene as this, the only reasonable thing to want to do is leave it. But the reality of the ghetto and the speaker's financial condition trap him there. "The Message" demonstrates the potential power of the simple image. Concrete and specific: "Rats in the front room, roaches in the back / junkies in the alley with a baseball bat." Such lines are direct, graphic, and effective.

If we pick up Ice Cube's "Alive on Arrival" where we last left it, we find these lines full of strong images:

> Coughin up blood on my hands and knees
> Then I heard "freeze nigger don't move"
> Yo, I didn't do a thing
> Didn't wanna go out like my man Rodney King
> Still got gaffled
> Internal bleeding as the bullet starts to travel
> Now I'm handcuffed
> Being asked information on my gang affiliation
> I don't bang, I rock the good rhymes
> And I'm a victim of neighborhood crime

The instinct of the rap/poet is to find events that are universally understood by the intended audience to carry the image to fruition. The lines "Yo I didn't do a thing / didn't want to go out like my man Rodney King" are a good example. The Rodney King beating, the subsequent trial, and the violence that greeted the verdict are read by different people in different ways. But implicit in this reference is an acknowledgement that the police are not likely to treat this victim kindly. The interrogation goes on despite the fact that we might be listening to our speaker die.

Images form the backbone of the rap/poem. They should be well constructed, varied, and evocative. When I consider the quality of the images presented in a rap/poem, I generally begin by asking:

1. How sophisticated is the rap/poet in conveying the images in this poem?
2. Are the images simple, complex, or a mix of the two?
3. Does the rap/poet employ effective use of language, as discussed above, to create powerful, evocative images?
4. Does the rap/poet make me see, feel, smell, and hear the details of the experiences he or she is writing about?
5. Are the images, in and of themselves, surprising? Do they make the common uncommon, the uncommon common?

TEXTURE

A key quality of effective rap/poems is texture, or complexity. This complexity might be achieved in a number of ways. When a rap/poem expresses interwoven or multiple story lines, includes complex metaphorical constructions, and uses intricate and complex language or imagery to convey multiple meanings, we might say it is textured.

We have said that rap/poetry is an art based on the local. Rap/poets generally write about what they know: their neighborhoods, cities, relationships, crews, and so forth. The ambitious rap/poet will often attempt to place this reality within the context of the larger world. To do this requires that the poet be able to draw comparisons, analyze world events, and identify trends. When successful, the poem will be a textured one.

Sometimes the element that complicates a simple meaning and transforms it into a textured message is a wonderful surprise at the end of an image, as in these lines from Eve's "Heaven Only Knows":

> Thought it was cute to flirt with older cats up in they face
> Didn't have a daddy so I put a daddy in his face

In those two lines, Eve reveals a system of substitution and loss that is profound. What began with us imagining a young girl acting above her age turns into the real tragedy that many young women must survive. The issue of fatherless families is framed in a brief but effective image. These are only two lines of an entire poem of other images that convey their own meaning.

This is how texture happens: when images build on each other, creating a layering effect. Tupac Shakur was a rap/poet of considerable skill in the use of texture. His poems were almost always textured. He, like many skilled rap/poets, experimented with ways of texturing his work. His "Dear Mama" comments not only on the implications of single-parent families but also on the rise of the "thug" identity:

> Now ain't nobody tell us it was fair
> No love from my daddy cause the coward wasn't there
> He passed away and I didn't cry, cause my anger
> wouldn't let me feel for a stranger
> They say I'm wrong and I'm heartless, but all along
> I was lookin for a father he was gone
> I hung around with the Thugs, and even though they sold drugs
> They showed a young brother love
> I moved out and started really hangin
> I needed money of my own so I started slangin
> I ain't guilty cause, even though I sell rocks
> It feels good puttin money in your mailbox
> I love payin rent when the rent's due
> I hope ya got the diamond necklace that I sent to you
> Cause when I was low you was there for me
> And never left me alone because you cared for me
> And I could see you comin home after work late
> You're in the kitchen tryin to fix us a hot plate
> Ya just workin with the scraps you was given
> And mama made miracles every Thanksgivin
> But now the road got rough, you're alone
> You're tryin to raise two bad kids on your own
> And there's no way I can pay you back
> But my plan is to show you that I understand
> You are appreciated

The texture of this poem depends on the unexpressed world that looks in on this story. Tupac takes into account the world that would negatively judge the crack slinging and gangsterism that the speaker in this rap/poem is talking about (albeit to help his mother make ends meet). Indeed, there is a play for our empathy. What does it mean to sell crack to help your mother? What would we do in the same circumstances, the poem seems to ask. Tupac knows we're looking in, because he addresses us directly: "And mama made miracles every Thanksgivin." That is for us. It signifies that in spite of all the hardship, love and family had their moments in the speaker's life.

Texture occurs when we learn or experience more than we expected at the outset. This is what we demand of poetry.

The highly textural nature of the best rap is one of the primary reasons we must pay attention to its aesthetical construction in the first place. Take, for example, this stanza from Scarface's "Mind Playing Tricks on Me":

> At night I can't sleep, I toss and turn
> Candle sticks in the dark, visions of bodies bein burned
> Four walls just starin at a nigga
> I'm paranoid, sleepin with my finger on the trigger
> My mother's always stressin I ain't livin right
> But I ain't going out without a fight

These six lines set the stage for the story being told in this poem. But they also contextualize the world of the "I." We are put on edge immediately. It is a reflection of the tension present in the poem. We learn right away the speaker hasn't slept, is lying in the dark, haunted by burning bodies. And presumably the shadows of this horrible scene are flickering on all four walls of his room. The speaker lies there with a gun in his hand, remembering his mother's admonition. But almost instantly the mood changes from despair to defiance: "I ain't going out without a fight." In the first six lines of this rap/poem, Scarface succeeds in establishing an introduction to his story and hence to its theme: namely, the consequences of a guilty conscience that is derived from less than ethical behavior.

But this excerpt, like the poem in its entirety, speaks to us on a deeper level. We can reflect on the significance of parenting and the way in which it operates in our adult lives. As an African American man, I am immediately empathetic precisely because I often feel pursued. Even though I presumably haven't the same cause to feel such paranoia, I understand it. I know it. At the moment the words filter through my brain, the speaker's paranoia seems no different from mine. As a result, this permits me to explore my psychological vulnerabilities. My weaknesses are flashed before my eyes and I might flinch. I'm afraid. I'm nervous. Not because I fear what Scarface fears, but because I fear some unnamed force just as he does.

These feelings, brought on from just these six lines, could catapult one into even deeper levels of self-exploration and contemplation of the larger world's impact on the self. Take the image of the poet lying in the bed with a gun in his hand. It's a defensive position. But we already sense the gun will do him no good. It's futile.

The best rap/poems, in a completely uncontrived and organic way, embody the very essence of texture. In less effective rap/poems, it is common to find lines that are effective in their superficial intent and even technically strong,

but that neither invite us nor engage us in their world. Rather, they seem unconscious of the potential power of the poet.

50 Cent is a talented rap/poet who doesn't always use texture. The images
in his popular "In Da Club" do not ask us to ponder their various meanings:

> When I pull up out front, you see the Benz on dubs
> When I roll 20 deep, it's 20 knives in the club
> Niggaz heard I fuck with Dre, now they wanna show me love
> When you sell like Eminem, and the hoes, they wanna fuck
> But homie ain't nuttin changed hoes down, G's up
> I see Xzibit in the cut—hey nigga roll that weed up
> If you watch how I move you'll mistake me for a player or pimp
> Been hit wit a few shells but I don't walk wit a limp (I'm aight)
> In the hood, in L.A. they sayin "50 you hot"
> They like me, I want them to love me like they love 'Pac
> But holla in New York them niggaz'll tell ya I'm loco
> And the plan is to put the rap game in a choke hold
> I'm fully focused man, my money on my mind
> Got a mill' out the deal and I'm still on the grind
> Now shawty said she feelin my style, she feelin my flow
> Her girlfriend willin to get bi and they ready to go (o-kay!)

The references to Tupac Shakur ("I want them to love me like they love
'Pac"), Dre, and Eminem do signify ambition and aspiration, but the writer
doesn't take it any further than that. The fact that "In Da Club," or any rap/
poem for that matter, is not significantly textured does not mean that the
poem cannot be effective as entertainment or as an announcement of saturation. And the fact that "In Da Club" rates low on our scale regarding texture
doesn't mean that this poet's other poems are also weak. 50 Cent gets at
texture with his controversial, satirical "How to Rob":

> Aiyyo the bottom line is I'ma crook with a deal
> If my record don't sell I'ma rob and steal
> You better recognize nigga I'm straight from the street
> These industry niggaz startin to look like somethin to eat
> I'll snatch Kim and tell Puff, "You wanna see her again?"
> Get your ass down to the nearest ATM
> I have dreams of fuckin an R&B bitch
> And I'll wake up early and bounce with all your shit
> When I apply pressure, son it aint even funny
> I'm about to stick Bobby for some of that Whitney money
> Brian McKnight, I can get that nigga anytime
> Have Keith sweatin starin down the barrel from my nine
> Since these Harlem World niggaz seem to all be fam

I put the gun to Cardin tell him, "Tell your man
Mason Betha, haha, come up of that watch now
I mean right now"
The only excuse for being broke is bein in jail
An entertainer can't make bail if he broke as hell
I'd rob ODB but that'd be a waste of time
Probably have to clap him run and toss the nine
I'd follow Fox in the drop for four blocks
Plottin to juice her for that rock Kurupt copped
What Jigga just sold like 4 mil? He got somethin to live for
Don't want no nigga puttin four thru that Bentley Coupe door
I'll man handle Mariah like "Bitch get on the ground"
You ain't with Tommy no more who gonna protect you now?
I been schemin' on Tone and Poke since they found me
Steve know not to wear that platinum shit around me
I'm a klepto nah for real son I'm sick
I'm bout to stick Slick Rick for all that old school shit
Right now I'm bent and when I get like this I don't think
About to make Stevie J take off that tight ass mink
I'll rob Pun without a gun snatch his piece then run
This nigga weigh 400 pounds, how he gon catch me son?

Using real names of popular rap artists supercharges this poem as texture
is built through Signifyin(g). The speaker in this rap/poem names Names as
a way of demonstrating ferocity and street-wise hardness. If he is capable of
the actions listed, he is indeed *bad*. John Henry bad.

As I've noted, texture or complexity is desired but not essential for a poem
to be successful. But we might also consider why a young, competitive rap/
poet might decide to withhold thoughtful observation and comment in a
work. There are at least four reasons why a rap/poem might be bereft of sufficient texture:

1. The poet isn't sufficiently aware of his or her relationship to the larger
   world.
2. The poet doesn't think enough of the listeners/readers to offer them
   multiple meanings.
3. The poet has decided that the best way of presenting the material is in a
   direct and nonmetaphorical way.
4. The poet has decided that the cost of texture is commercial success and
   chooses popularity.

I want to develop further that last point. The "deeper" or more textured
the poem, the more likely the number of listeners will decrease. The concept

of "diminishing returns" is apropos here. It is in this territory that "blowing up" or bonafide commercial success seems to have a negative effect on many talented rap/poets. If you think about it, this phenomenon makes sense. It isn't that the listeners are incapable of comprehending complex poems, but rather, that texture itself is a kind of preference. Many people come to rap thinking of it solely as music. Consequently, heavily textured poems are not valued over beat and the energy of the performance. A stanza from Jay Z's "Moment of Clarity" speaks directly to this point:

> Music business hate me cause the industry ain't make me
> Hustlers and boosters embrace me and the music I be makin
> I dumbed down for my audience to double my dollars
> They criticized me for it yet they all yell "HOLLA!"
> If skills sold, truth be told, I'd probably be
> lyrically, Talib Kweli
> Truthfully I wanna rhyme like Common Sense
> But I did five mill'—I ain't been rhymin like Common since
> When your cents got that much in common
> And you been hustlin since, your inception
> Fuck perception go with what makes sense
> Since I know what I'm up against
> We as rappers must decide what's most important
> And I can't help the poor if I'm one of them
> So I got rich and gave back, to me that's the win/win
> So next time you see the homey and his rims spin
> Just know my mind is workin just like them . . .
> . . . rims, that is

In particular, the lines "If skills sold, truth be told, I'd probably be / lyrically, Talib Kweli / Truthfully I wanna rhyme like Common Sense / But I did five mil—I ain't been rhyming like Common since" hit the mark. Talib Kweli and Common have a reputation for being (and are) quality rap/poets. Their work is generally well crafted and highly textured. Jay Z has that capacity and occasionally demonstrates it (as he does in "Moment of Clarity"), but he reveals that should a rap/poet commit to texture, he or she is less likely to make as much money.

Suffice it to say, then, texture offers up a multiplicity of meanings within the space of single poem. Texture is the reason a poem by Tupac will cause deeper reverberations within us for a longer period of time than one by, say, Chingy.

Because of rap's popularity and the ever present hip hop culture it speaks for, rap consumers are perhaps more diverse in terms of gender, age, class, race, and ethnicity than any other market segment. That diversity has its pluses and minuses. One plus is that young people are sharing experiences across all manner of borders. One minus is that as the market has grown, the consumers have become less demanding of the poets. Indeed, many ardent consumers of rap do not know and might not believe that it is an African American art form (or at least has its roots there); consequently, the issues of struggle and oppositionality that would naturally fit into that art are not necessarily expected, which makes it possible then to create rap/poems that are derivative, simplistic, and worst of all, demeaning.

I refer to Little Brother and their chorus to the poem "The Listening":

> This is a message for our people chasing benjamins
> With real rhymes and skills they believing in
> Keeping them bad tapes rolling like Michelin
> it don't matter, cause niggaz ain't listening
> They ain't listening, they thinkin bout they timbalands
> They say the shit we talk about ain't interestin
> We got a better chance of blowing up in Switzerland
> Holla if you hear it cause niggaz ain't listening

Little Brother knows that more rap/poets are increasingly being swayed by the money; and in this mostly cynical excerpt, they encourage it because "niggaz ain't listening." In this way, the group acknowledges the economic futility in choosing the road of highly textured and complex rap/poems. They seem to be saying that if most people are simply dancing to the beat, it really doesn't matter what the rap/poem is saying or how well it is constructed. Little Brother is also reminding us that they will not compromise in spite of the fact that they too will lose listeners/readers.

Still, I find it very useful to calculate the complexity of a given rap/poem based on the multiple subjects and issues referred. When a poet is able to combine complexity with clarity and does so in a viable structure, that poem rises in quality. I suggest that reader/listeners consider the texture of a rap/ poem by identifying how referential a poet is. Does the poet refer to other rap/poets or rap/poems? Does the rap/poet refer to historical, political, or economic realities that complicate the effectiveness of the poem? Is the rap/poem dialogic; does it speak to other rap/poets or respond to other rap/poems?

MEANING

Textured rap/poems convey many different meanings over the course of the journey they take us on. Each image, often each line of a poem, provides its own reason for being, namely to play its part in the story that is being told and to add to the clarity of the central meaning of the whole.

Each rap/poem, whether textured or not, has a singular meaning at its core. In a way, the multiple meanings (that are generated from texture) that might be apparent in a poem are actually performing in service to one central meaning. The challenge is to discern that central meaning as a primary way of determining the poem's significance. For example, a poem that has a message like "There's no way to be successful in life unless you are a gangster and are willing to rob people" has less significance to me than a poem that expresses its meaning as "Life's a struggle, but if you prepare yourself and learn all you can, you can be successful." But that's just me. I will nearly always opt for the positive message over the dark or destructive.

Obviously, this is not to say that the first example doesn't represent a feeling that some people have. And it also doesn't mean that the "gangster is the only way" message can't be a better-written poem than the "prepare yourself" poem. I simply prefer the second message. This, in many ways, becomes a determining factor in establishing a personal hierarchy of preference. For example, as I've said, I think all objectifications of women, all gratuitous violent images, all use of homophobic language, and all outright racist statements, unless employed to interrogate their use and existence, work against a poem's quality and significance.

Great language, rich, saturated images, and interesting structure are important components of a successful rap/poem. But I want to know why the poet wrote this particular piece. What is the point? Sometimes, when I finally figure it out, I am put off by it. I might feel, as I often do, that this poet has squandered space, time, and talent to offer up only a scatological or inconsequential message. But I still want to know it. Sometimes I'm confounded to the point where I am almost willing to admit that a particular piece simply has no meaning. Almost. I soothe myself by accepting *that* as meaning, if you follow me. The privilege of speaking without meaning is, perhaps, to a young African American man, full of meaning.

Discovering meaning in rap/poetry is not as hard or as easy as it may seem. Too many listeners of rap don't particularly look for meaning; consequently, their initial attempts to do it are almost amusing. The first attempts to discern meaning in a poem almost always take us to the most obvious, the most literal. Sometimes this is an effective path to meaning, but often it isn't. Poets often submerge meaning beneath a myriad of images and complex texture. But, of course, there are also too many listeners who simply assume that most rap is meaningless.

I believe that it is worth it to delve into even the simplest, most commercial rap to discern its raison d'etre before celebrating or condemning it. Near the end of my course on the poetry of rap, I often ask: "What is the common thread that connects all rap/poetry?" My answer is that it is not politics, not beliefs or values, not even the stories (as diverse as they are), but rather, the sheer act of self-expression. This is why we should be careful not to generalize about rap. Rap/poetry is an amalgamation of individual spirits speaking, expressing themselves. In this society, that is an important thing. It may be sad or dangerous, but it is important. We should care about the values being expressed, just as we should about the loneliness, despair, and fear in rap/poetry.

Often, when a rap/poem causes me to cringe, it is because I don't like the particular language that is being used. But more likely it is that once I've figured out what is being said, I don't like what it means. In the context of poetry, it doesn't matter whether I cringe or not. Self-expression is its own reward. The truth is that the range of meaning that is exhibited in rap/poems can be traced to how this society nurtures and educates its youth. The range of meaning can also be traced to the images of hope and possibility they have been exposed to relative to those of despair and degradation.

By talking about meaning, I intend to say that rap/poets have a responsibility to mean what they say and to be accountable for that in some artistic and aesthetic way. But it is also important to note that many of them speak to us in an authentic language and reveal to us truths about their experiences.

Too often, other than the language, it is the meaning of the poem that excites or disturbs us. In effect, rap/poetry provides answers to the questions of contemporary urban life. What is a man? What is a woman? What is virtue? Marriage? Justice? Childhood? God? Family? Rap provides answers to these questions from a particular perspective. The best examples of rap/poetry leave a residue of meaning that continues to occupy our minds after the poem is over.

And once understood, a rap/poem's meaning can be quite simple. J-Live's "Satisfied?" can be useful here as an example. The poem is rich with well-constructed and saturated images and fairly bursting with meaning. He says if freedom is what you seek, you won't find it through money or through the political system. You especially won't find it through the government, because even after the tragedy of September 11, 2001, the system of American oppression still targeted inner-city black people. However, the central meaning of this rap/poem is something more fundamental than those already mentioned. Rap/poets who are conscious of the central meaning of their poems will often reveal it to their readers/listeners, as J-Live does here:

> Hey yo
> Lights, camera, tragedy, comedy, romance
> You better dance from your fighting stance
> Or you'll never have a fighting chance
> In the rat race

Where the referee's son started way in advance
But still you livin' the American Dream
Silk PJ's, sheets and down pillows
Who the fuck would wanna wake up?
You got it good like hot sex after the break up
Your four car garage it's just more space to take up
You even bought your mom a new whip scrap the jalopy
Thousand dollar habit, million dollar hobby
You a success story everybody wanna copy
But few work for it, most get jerked for it
If you think that you could ignore it, you're ignorant
A fat wallet still never made a man free
They say to eat good, yo, you gotta swallow your pride
But debt that game plan, I'm not satisfied

The poor get worked, the rich get richer
The world gets worse, do you get the picture?
The poor gets dead, the rich get depressed
The ugly get mad, the pretty get stressed
The ugly get violent, the pretty get gone
The old get stiff, the young get stepped on
Whoever told you that it was all good lied
So throw your fists up if you not satisfied

Are you satisfied?
I'm not satisfied

Hey yo, the air's still stale
The anthrax got my Ole Earth wearin' a mask and gloves to get a meal
I know a older guy that lost twelve close peeps on 9-1-1
While you kickin' up punchlines and puns
Man fuck that shit, this is serious biz
By the time Bush is done, you won't know what time it is
If it's war time or jail time, time for promises
And time to figure out where the enemy is
The same devils that you used to love to hate
They got you so gassed and shook now, you scared to debate
The same ones that traded books for guns
Smuggled drugs for funds
And had fun lettin' off forty-one
But now it's all about NYPD caps
And Pentagon bumper stickers
But yo, you still a nigga
It ain't right them cops and them firemen died
The shit is real tragic, but it damn sure ain't magic

It won't make the brutality disappear
It won't pull equality from behind your ear
It won't make a difference in a two-party country
If the president cheats, to win another four years
Now don't get me wrong, there's no place I'd rather be
The grass ain't greener on the other genocide
But tell Huey Freeman don't forget to cut the lawn
And uproot the weeds
Cuz I'm not satisfied

All this genocide
Is not justified
Are you satisfied?
I'm not satisfied

Yo, poison pushers making paper off of pipe dreams
They turned hip-hop to a get-rich-quick scheme
The rich minorities control the gov'ment
But they would have you believe we on the same team
So where you stand, huh?
What do you stand for?
Sit your ass down if you don't know the answer
Serious as cancer, this jam demands your undivided attention
Even on the dance floor
Grab the bull by the horns, the bucks by the antlers
Get yours, what're you sweatin' the next man for?
Get down, feel good to this, let it ride
But until we all free, I'll never be satisfied

Are you satisfied?
(whoever told you that it was all good lied)
I'm not satisfied
(Throw your fists up if you not satisfied)
Are you satisfied?
(Whoever told you that it was all good lied)
I'm not satisfied
(So throw your fists up)
(So throw your fists up)
(Throw your fists up)

Sandwiched between the images and observations, J-Live asks two questions: "So where you stand, huh? What do you stand for?" These questions lead us to the central meaning: it is important to stand for something. On my scale of measurement, this meaning would rank high. "Satisfied?" is a well-textured rap/poem. It takes us on a circuitous journey. But in the end, we realize the poet has tried to motivate us to think and perhaps has inspired us to act.

Eminem is another rap/poet whose work is nearly always meaningful. He rides the line of decorum and offensiveness with the best of poets. He is a disturber, a trickster of the highest order. He seeks the space to say things that upset and challenge his listeners. Sometimes he does this with violent images and sometimes with a penetrating incursion into the American psyche. In "White America," we are exposed to an honest take on his own success:

> I never woulda dreamed in a million years I'd see
> so many motherfuckin people, who feel like me
> Who share the same views and the same exact beliefs
> It's like a fuckin ARMY marchin in back of me
> So many lives I touched, so much anger aimed
> in no particular direction, just sprays and sprays
> And straight through your radio waves, it plays and plays
> 'til it stays stuck in your head, for days and days
> Who woulda thought; standin in this mirror bleachin my hair
> with some peroxide, reachin for a t-shirt to wear
> that I would catapult to the forefront of rap like this?
> How could I predict my words would have an impact like this?
> I must've struck a chord with somebody up in the office
> Cause Congress keep tellin me, I ain't causin nuthin but problems
> And now they're sayin I'm in trouble with the government—I'm lovin it!
> I shoveled shit all my life, and now I'm dumpin it on
>
> White America! I could be one of your kids
> White America! Little Eric looks just like this
> White America! Erica loves my shit
> I go to TRL; look how many hugs I get!
>
> Look at these eyes, baby blue, baby just like yourself
> If they were brown Shady lose, Shady sits on the shelf
> But Shady's cute, Shady knew Shady's dimples would help
> Make ladies swoon baby (ooh baby!) Look at my sales
> Let's do the math—if I was black, I woulda sold half
> I ain't have to graduate from Lincoln High School to know that
> But I could rap, so fuck school, I'm too cool to go back
> Gimme the mic, show me where the fuckin studio's at
> When I was underground, no one gave a fuck I was white
> No labels wanted to sign me, almost gave up I was like
> Fuck it—until I met Dre, the only one to look past
> Gave me a chance and I lit a FIRE up under his ass

Helped him get back to the top, every fan black that I got
was probably his in exchange for every white fan that he's got
Like damn; we just swapped—sittin back lookin at shit, wow
I'm like my skin is it startin to work to my benefit now? It's . . .

See the problem is, I speak to suburban kids
who otherwise woulda never knew these words exist
Whose moms probably woulda never gave two squirts of piss
'til I created so much motherfuckin turbulence!
Straight out the tube, right into your living rooms I came
And kids flipped, when they knew I was produced by Dre
That's all it took, and they were instantly hooked right in
And they connected with me too because I looked like them
That's why they put my lyrics up under this microscope
Searchin with a fine tooth comb, it's like this rope
waitin to choke; tightenin around my throat
Watchin me while I write this, like I don't like this (Nope!)
All I hear is: lyrics, lyrics, constant controversy, sponsors working
round the clock to try to stop my concerts early, surely
Hip-Hop was never a problem in Harlem only in Boston
After it bothered the fathers of daughters startin to blossom
So now I'm catchin the flack from these activists when they raggin
Actin like I'm the first rapper to smack a bitch or say faggot, shit!
Just look at me like I'm your closest pal
The poster child, the motherfuckin spokesman now for . . .

So to the parents of America
I am the derringer aimed at little Erica to attack her character
The ringleader of this circus of worthless pawns
Sent to lead the march right up to the steps of Congress
and piss on the lawns of the White House
To burn the {flag} and replace it with a Parental Advisory sticker
To spit liquor in the faces of this democracy of hypocrisy
Fuck you Ms. Cheney! Fuck you Tipper Gore!
Fuck you with the free-est of speech
this Divided States of Embarrassment will allow me to have
Fuck you!
I'm just playin America, you know I love you

I'm not sure what central meaning you might discern from this rap/poem,
but for me, it is that young white people, despite their wide protestations,
see and can admit that race (particularly the black/white paradigm) is still a
factor in America and that they benefit from it. This is one of those "truths"
that people of color accept that many white people will challenge. It takes a

Michael Moore or, in this case, an Eminem to confirm to black people that they aren't crazy or hallucinating. Again, the quality of this meaning is high.

Sometimes a central meaning will be deeply hidden within the context of the local, where only those truly in the know will be able to discern its central meaning. Of course, many people who live within the world of hip hop will seek out hidden meanings at the slightest hint of their existence. It is, after all, the information age. And hip hop minutiae has its value as anyone who has ever gotten caught up in an argument with an avid rap fan will attest.

In the rap/poem "Kill That Noise" by MC Shan, we witness a battle between KRS-One of Boogie Down Productions and the Juice Crew of which MC Shan was a member. To insiders, it is obvious that it is written in answer to BDP's "South Bronx." "South Bronx" in turn was written in response to an earlier MC Shan poem, "The Bridge." Essentially the two rap/poets are arguing over claims of where hip hop started, in Queensbridge Brooklyn or the South Bronx. Shan repeats KRS-One's refrain "South Bronx" with the simple closing phrase "kill that noise."

"Kill That Noise" is a poem of braggadocio and warning executed in 1988 in a less menacing way than it might have been were it written in the mid-1990s. What might on the surface seem simple and uncomplicated is made complex by insider information. Consequently, the meaning of this rap/poem will be different for different listeners:

> Rhyming is a thing that I do at will
> Be glad to rock a party just to prove my skill
> J-u-ice is what I'm gaining
> With a style so fresh that it's self-explaining
> Never bite a rhyme, I don't live that way
> But when I get dissed, violators pay
> I'm a crowd motivator, MC annihilator
> Never front the move cause I'm not a perpetrator
> I don't really mind bein criticized
> But those who try to make fame on my name—die
> Rhymes of all styles, all categories
> From fresh freestyles to real fly stories
> This jam is dedicated to you and your boys
> And if you knew what I knew, then you'd kill that noise
>
> (Devastating to your ear)
>
> I devastate the crowd while the record spins
> So call, competitors have no wins
> I laugh at MC's who call me wack
> You ordered, and now I'm gonna serve you, Jack

We're respected by all, treated just like kings
How could you have the nerve to say such things?
If you knew at the time what you were saying
You wouldn't be on your knees—praying
You gotta understand I'm not the average MC
At the first sign of trouble grab the mic and flee
Grab the mic, plug in the beat box jacks
Prepare for the battle, then proceed to wax
Takes much time I feel is ample
To deafen an MC, to make an example
This goes for all sucker MC chumps
Who hear my name, and suddenly Kool-Aid pumps
So if you're thinkin 'bout dissin me, better think twice
Cause next time, brother, I won't be so nice
You can come all alone or bring all your boys
But if you knew what I knew, then you'd kill that noise

(South Bronx)
Kill that, kill that noise

In rap/poetry, meaning can be discerned in a variety of ways. A rap/poet can present meaning as an expressed part of the poem. Or meaning can be offered through the poem's texture. The fascinating thing about meaning occurs during the process of trying to figure it out. It forces us through the territory of image, language, saturation, and texture. I suspect that what happens most often is that we discern a meaning different from the one intended by the rap/poet. And this, I think, is natural.

In the early days of rap, MCs would often call rapping "shooting the gift." And I do believe that rap is a gift that young urban folks give to society. Society has often misunderstood it. Castigated it. In fact, society has responded with at least as much fear of rap music and its poetry as it has love. But art, in the form of self-expression, really is a gift. And, as with any gift, the receiver gets to do with it what he or she will. So the idea that each poem has a meaning should be placed against the idea that our understanding of that meaning might be different from someone else's, including the rap/poet's.

In "White Man'z World," Makaveli (Tupac Shakur) uses a personal reflection combined with a racial and political analysis of American culture to lead up to his meaning, which can be found in his final stanza:

"You go bustin your fist against a stone wall,
you're not usin your brain. That's what the white man wants you to do.
Look at you! What makes you ashamed of bein black?"

(Nuttin but love for you my sister)
Might even know how hard it is (no doubt)
Bein a woman, a black woman at that? (no doubt)
Shit—in this white man's world
Sometimes we overlook the fact that we be ridin hard on our sisters
we don't be knowin the pain we be causin (in this white man's world)
In this white man's world . . I ain't sayin I'm innocent in all this
I'm just sayin (in this white man's world)
This song is for y'all
For all those times that I messed up or we messed up

Dear sister, got me twisted up in prison I miss ya
Cryin lookin at my niece's and my nephew's picture
They say don't let this cruel world get ya, kinda suspicious
Swearin one day you might leave me, for somebody that's richer
Twist the cap off the bottle, I take a sip and see tomorrow
Gotta make if I have to beg or borrow
Readin love letters; late night, locked down and quiet
If brothers don't receive they mail best believe we riot
Eatin Jack-Mack, starin at walls of silence
inside this cage where they captured all my rage and violence
In time I learned a few lessons, never fall for riches
Apologies to my TRUE sisters; far from bitches
Help me raise my black nation reparations are due, it's true
Caught up in this world I took advantage of you
So tell the babies how I love them, precious boys and girls
Born black in this white man's world—and all I heard was

Who, knows what tomorrow brings
In this world, where everyone's blind
And where to go, no matter how far I'll find
To let you know, that you're not alone

Only thing they ever did wrong (YES, YES)
was bein born black, in this white man's world (NO DOUBT)
(All my ghetto motherfuckers be proud to be black and be PROUD)
All my little black seeds, born black in this white man's world
(to have this shit like this, cause ain't NOBODY got it like this)
(All these motherfuckers wanna be like us, they all wanna be like us)
(To be the have-nots, all hail)
(God bless the child that can hold his own, no motherfuckin doubt)

Bein born with less I must confess only adds on to the stress
Two gunshots to my homie's head, dyed in his vest
Shot him to death and left him bleedin for his family to see

I pass his casket gently askin, is there heaven for G's?
My homeboy's doin life, his baby momma be stressin
Sheddin tears when her son, finally ask that questions
Where my daddy at? Mama why we live so poor?
Why you cryin? Heard you late night through my bedroom door
Now do you love me mama? Whitey keep on callin me nigga?
Get my weight up with my hate and pay 'em back when I'm bigger
And still thuggin in this jail cell, missin my block
Hearin brothers screamin all night, wishin they'd stop
Proud to be black but why we act like we don't love ourselves
Don't look around busta (you sucka) check yourselves
Know what it MEANS to be black, whether a man or girl
We still strugglin, in this white man's world

It is perhaps an excuse for anyone who finds himself in prison, but it is entirely possible that the forlorn and melancholic reality of that existence is proof enough that "we still strugglin, in this white man's world." This poem and many others that are discussed here demonstrate that the rap/poets are capable of metaphysical contemplation. They are as occupied as any group of poets with the nature of life, freedom, honor, love, and passion.

Sometimes meaning comes in the form of a parable. KRS-One's "Love's Gonna Getcha (Material Love)" provides a perfect example of a rap/poet who is conscious of the power of words and the poet's role as teacher, guide, and griot. In fact, among the best of rap/poets you will find an elevated consciousness of both their responsibilities and connection to their presumed audiences. Caught at once trying to present moral, ethical, and political advice while appealing to the most base urges of the disenfranchised and marginalized underclass, it is a difficult place to find oneself. And we find all manner of facility and lack thereof as poets try to perform in this territory. But KRS-One has been one of the best at finding that balance:

I'm in junior high with a b plus grade,
at the end of the day I don't hit the arcade,
I walk from school to my moms apartment,
I got to tell the suckas everyday "don't start it,"
cause where I'm at if your soft your lost,
to say on course means to roll with force,
a boy named Rob is chillin in a Benz,
in front of my building with the rest of his friends,
I give him a pound, oh I mean I shake his hand,
he's the neighborhood drug dealer, my man,
I go upstairs and hug my mother,
kiss my sister, and punch my brother,

I sit down on my bed to watch some tv,
(machine gun fire) do my ears deceive me,
Nope, that's the fourth time this week,
another fast brother shot dead in the street,
the very next day while I'm off to class,
my moms goes to work cold busting her ass,
my sisters cute but she got no gear,
I got three pairs of pants and with my brother I share,
see there in school see I'm made a fool,
with one and a half pair of pant you aint cool,
but there's no dollars for nothing else,
I got beans, rice, and bread on my shelf,
every day I see my mother struggling,
now its time I've got to do something,
I look for work I get dissed like a jerk,
I do odd jobs and come home like a slob,
so here comes Rob he's cold and shivery,
he gives me two hundred for a quick delivery,
I do it once, I do it twice,
now there's steak with the beans and rice,
my mother's nervous but she knows the deal,
my sister's gear now has sex appeal,
my brothers my partner and we're getting paper,
three months later we run our own caper,
my family's happy everything is new,
now tell me what the fuck am I supposed to do,

that's why, (loves gonna get you)
(loves gonna get you)(loves gonna get you)(loves gonna get you)
you fall in love with your chain,
you fall in love with your car,
loves gonna sneak right up and snuff you from behind,
so I want you to check the story out as we go down the line,
(loves gonna get you)(loves gonna get you)(loves gonna get you)

money's flowing, everything is fine,
got myself an uzi and my brother a nine,
business is boomin' everything is cool,
I pull about a g a week fuck school,
a year goes by and I begin to grow,
not in height but juice and cash flow,
I pick up my feet and begin to watch tv,
cause now I got other people working for me,
I got a 55 inch television you know,
and every once in awhile I hear just say no,

or the other commercial I love,
is when they say, this is your brain on drugs,
I pick up my remote control and just turn,
cause with that bullshit I'm not concerned,
see me and my brother jump in the BM,
driving around our territory again,
I stop at the light like a superstar,
and automatic weapons cold sprayed my car,
I hit the accelerator scared as fuck,
and drove one block to find my brother was hit,
he wasn't dead but the blood was pouring,
and all I could think about was war and,
later I found that it was Rob and his crew,
now tell me what the fuck am I supposed to do,

ya know that's why, (loves gonna get you)
(loves gonna get you)(loves gonna get you)(love loves gonna get you)
(loves gonna get you)(loves gonna get you)(loves gonna get you)
(love loves gonna get you)(loves gonna get you)
that word love is very very serious(loves gonna get you)
very addictive

my brothers out of it, but I'm still in it,
on top of that I'm in it to win it,
I can't believe that Rob would diss me,
that faggot, that punk, he's soft a sissy,
I'm driving around now with three of my guys,
the war is on and I'm on the rise,
we rolled right up to his favorite hang out,
said hello and then the bullets rang out,
some fired back so we took cover,
and all I could think about was my brother,
Rob jumped up and began to run,
busting shots hoping to hit someone,
so I just stopped, and let off three shots,
two hit him and one hit a cop,
I threw the gun down and began to shout,
come on I got him it's time to break out,
but as we ran there were the boys in blue,
pointing their guns at my four man crew,
they shot down one, they shot down two,
now tell me what the fuck am I supposed to do,

The city scene—along with its culture of money and material things—gets
fully rendered here. But at its heart, there is a deeper question that speaks to the

moral and ethical dilemma. "You tell me," KRS-One seems to be saying. "Given that the world is the way it is, white racism the way it is, my chance of success as an African American man in this society seems already to be moot. Given that, what would you do? What would you have me do?" The answer to that question is the meaning of this rap/poem. In addition, I think he does an interesting thing in regards to redefining love. He gives us a new image of love—love for family as something that has the potential to destroy. This is in direct opposition to the mainstream idea that family always provides strength. In this situation, love for family can cause you to compromise your morals and values.

Jean Grae, in "Block Party," comes right out and tells you that her poem is an "Editorial, about the state of things, state of mind and state of being / What the fuck is goin on?"

> [Verse One]
> Listen
> I don't wanna preach or come off bitter, this is a commentary auditory
> Editorial, about the state of things, state of mind and state of being
> What the fuck is goin on? How the fuck we gonna make it out?
> It's hectic, from asbestos filled classrooms
> to the stench of death that's still in New York
> The air is thick with it, but it reaches further
> Like the world murder rate
> Circulate, cultivate your mind and soul, your heart and your body
> So stagnant; niggaz, get off your block and travel
> Stop actin like your flesh is metal and your hood's a magnet
> We need to globalize, further spread on this earth
> to appreciate the full value of individual worth
> To realize how ridiculous the thought of ownership is
> and protectin your turf—that's bullshit man
> That's how we got colonized
> Missionaries create foreign schools and change the native way & thinkin
> So in ten years, we can have a foreign Columbine
> in some small village in the Amazon, c'mon man
>
> [Chorus]
> You need to get out your house, get off your block, and see somethin
> Go do somethin, go CHANGE somethin, or else we fall for nothin
> You need to, travel the world
> And when you come back, tell your girl and your girl and your girl . .
> and your man and your man and your man . . you understand?
> So spread the word
>
> [Verse Two]
> It's every man for himself

That's why the black community is lackin in wealth, there's no unity
We soon to be chillin with rich white folk
and that means that we made it
Let our kids go hungry before our wardrobe is outdated
Rap careers are drug related, ballplayers, we need more lawyers
More housin and job created, why we waitin for it to be given?
We need to get up, and get out, and make our own livin
Instead of just makin more, inner-city children
More doctors in your building, righteous cops next door
If the system's corrupt, then change it
Fought for the right to vote, don't even use it
Forget electoral winnin
The way the world's goin, we in the ninth inning
Heh, and we still aren't up to bat
Niggaz is happy just to have the rights to sit on the bench
Like floor seats is alright, and that's as far as we reach
Materialistic values, not morals, that's what we teach
I see it in the youth, hungry for fame and money
Not for knowledge and pursuit of the truth
Pick up a book or a newspaper
Take a free class in politics or human behavior
We need to stop actin victimized, it's like we're day-walkin blind
Open your eyes, there's a whole world out there

[Chorus]

[Verse Three]
And you don't have to agree, or just be happy
Content and lose your hunger, push further
Cause I don't believe that pipe dreams exist
The world is what you make it, your life is all that you got
So take it to the limit
Why would you deny your spirit growth and happiness?
And if your peoples hold you back, they not your peoples at all
You know the, misery cliche
Ladies, know your worth; the way we givin it up
We might as well auction ourselves on eBay, to the lowest bidder
So what if his dough is better? Money doesn't make the man
Maybe self-sufficiency would better make you understand
Let's get it together
There's so much promise and it's just goin to waste
We turn crude, lack of class, lack of taste
And trust, they laughin at us
It's slow genocide
And I don't care how many bottles of Cristal you pop

> It won't un-expose you as a known pedophile
> Native child, runnin wild, to the ends of the earth
> I'll see y'all at the last hundred miles, bet

This highly textured rap/poem makes its meaning clear in a very direct way. Located in the chorus is the rap/poem's meaning. Grae challenges men and women to change themselves. To grow.

In order to locate meaning in rap/poetry, the reader/listener must spend the time necessary to find it. This is complicated by the fact that once found, sometimes the meaning isn't worthy of the effort. But when it is, having an intimate knowledge of a well-constructed, ambitious, and intelligent rap/poem can be inspirational.

When the Professor would finish his long, nonsensical ramblings and the night air hung heavy, he would stare at us with a smile that seemed to be waiting for our acknowledgement that we had understood what he'd said. But we hadn't. We just stared back. And then, after thirty seconds or a minute of awkward ghetto silence, he'd raise his hand, smiling all the while, and say goodbye. When he disappeared around the corner, we'd laugh. We'd try to remember the words he'd used. But we'd never actually try to figure out what he was saying. His entire effort at communication was lost on us. When we don't make the effort to decipher the meaning of many of the most significant rap/poems, we lose our ability to understand the growth, stresses, and possibilities of our society.

STRUCTURE, FORM, AND RHYTHM

When it comes to structure, we are confronted with a number of interesting questions as it pertains to understanding rap/poetry. The language, the images, and their meanings rely on some system of organization, or structure, to bring them together and make a complete rap/poem. There are at least two ways we might think about rap/poetry's structure. One way would be to measure the length of the lines of a given poem and compare them against each other in order to discern a structure. The other would be to observe the construction of the rhyme, paying attention to the frequency and complexity of the rhyme scheme to understand its structure. One might use both techniques together but, as I will explain more fully a bit later, I am partial to the latter technique.

To measure the length of a line of a rap/poem, it is helpful to think of each line as a collection of accented and unaccented syllables. A line is a rhythmic percussion of stresses and pauses. Indeed, if we take one line of a poem and break the words into syllables, we are able to distinguish between those that are accented, or stressed, and those that are not.

Using "^" to note unaccented and "+" to note accented syllables, we can analyze a line from KRS-One's "Love's Gonna Getcha" this way:

```
^ + /    ^ +    / ^ + / ^ + /  ^ +
A boy / named Rob / is chil / lin in / a Benz
```

This process for analyzing lines of poetry is called scansion. The accented and unaccented syllables create structure in two ways. The first is the dominant pattern of stresses being used. The pattern shown above makes use of "iambs." An iamb is a unit made up of an unaccented syllable followed by an accented syllable. These units in a line of poetry are referred to as "feet," and there are different kinds of feet, based on the pattern of unaccented and accented syllables. Iambs are the basic units of most ordinary speech in the English language. But you will also encounter patterns made up of an accented syllable followed by an unaccented syllable; these are called trochees. Or you might find a pattern made up of two unaccented syllables followed by an accented syllable; these are called anapests.

The second way of creating structure is by using "meter." The dominant meter being used in a poem is determined by the type of feet and how many of them there are in a line. Because the above line from "Love's Gonna Getcha" has five iambic feet, it is said to have been written in iambic pentameter. If a line has four iambic feet, it is iambic tetrameter, and a line with six iambic feet is iambic hexameter.

This yields an interesting way of looking at rap/poems. To understand more about their structure, let's look at some lines from Lil Kim's "This Is Who I Am." Readers may not all agree on where some of the accents fall, but usually a pattern can be found in most of the lines.

```
        ^ + /    ^ +  / ^ + / + ^  /  + ^  /   ^ +
1. A bout / five feet / e ven, / kind a / small in / the waist
        1 /    2    /   3  /  4  /   5   /   6


        ^ +   /   ^ +  /   ^ +  / ^ + /   ^ +
2. Rap's sex / sym bol, / real pret / ty in / the face
        1   /    2   /    3   /  4  /   5


        ^ +  / ^ + / ^ + /  ^ +  /  ^ +  /    ^ ^ +
3. So what / I got / e ven / big ger / tit ties / than the lakes
        1  / 2 /  3  /   4   /   5   /    6


  + ^ ^  / + ^  / + ^  /  + ^ ^   /  + ^  /   ^ ^ +
```

4. Still a so / phist i / ca ted / la dy with / mil lions / in the safe
        1   /   2   /   3   /   4   with /   5   /   6

        +   /   ^ + /   ^ ^ +   /   ^ ^ +
5. Switch / up flows / like I switch / up my clothes
        1   /   2   /   3   /   4

        + /   ^ ^ +   /   ^ ^ +   /   ^ ^ +
6. More / than Wilt Cham / ber lain switched / up his hoes
        1 /   2   /   3   /   4

       + ^ / ^ + / ^ + /   ^ ^ + /   ^ ^ +
7. I'm a / per fec / tion ist, / got ta stay / on my toes
        1 /   2   /   3   /   4   /   5

       + ^ /.   ^ +   /   ^ ^ +   /   ^ ^ +
8. An y / thing goes / when you play / with the pro's
        1 /   2   /   3   /   4

It is important to note that many combinations of syllables are available to the poet. For example, line 4 ends with "in the safe," which is an anapest, two unaccented syllables and an accented one. And, as I said, there are other kinds of feet, such as trochees, spondees, pyrrhics, and so forth. In this way, the poet has many ways to change up the rhythm of a poem. Notice how Lil Kim uses anapests in other lines and as a final point at the end of line 8.

After a poem has been "scanned," we can talk about the details of construction from a line measurement standpoint. When I first began teaching the poetry of rap, I spent a considerable amount of time working with my students to scan rap/poems in this manner. My purpose was twofold. I wanted them to see that many rap/poems were constructed in a traditional way: that they used iambs, for example, and that the lines they created were constructed in a fairly classical way. That is, the lines were generally written in pentameter, trimeter, tetrameter, and hexameter. I wanted them to see the rhythm of a poem, not in the music that surrounded it, but in the actual way the words were set together in a line.

I still think there is some marginal merit in this approach, but the information it yields, particularly in rap/poetry, is severely limited. What it does reveal is a sense of the rap/poet's self-consciousness about line construction. When you discover a poet who seems to understand that there is iambic structure in the rap/poem and manipulates and modulates that structure for the good of the poem, it is greatly satisfying. That is the thing about iambs. They are enormously satisfying. They capture the sound of contemporary speech. People converse quite naturally in iambs, and a poet's natural voice is derived from the sound of those around her or him, although not necessarily always in pentameter. Indeed most rap/poets seem to gravitate to tetrameter or trimeter more often than pentameter.

But this is a mathematical way of discerning structure in rap and not as interesting to me as the second way of looking at rap/poetic structure. Also, the question of the poet's intention is key here. Does the rap/poet know and understand the nature of language and poetic forms to intentionally create a line of iambic pentameter, or is it all accidental? Scansion is less meaningful if we suspect the poet isn't in control of line construction.

One problem in scanning rap/poems arises because it is difficult to obtain a printed version that is identical to the way the rap/poet wrote it. When these poems *are* printed, they are often presented without the poet's final approval; consequently, we are left not being sure whether a line break (where a line of poetry ends) is intentional and done by the poet or by a typist. We must be confident the line breaks in a printed rap/poem are intentional before we can trust the results of scansion. Most times, we can sense line breaks, as in the Lil Kim poem above, by observing the rhyme. In this book, we have accepted the line breaks as they are presented in publication, but when it comes to scansion, our uncertainty about the poet's intention prevents us from completely trusting this form of analysis.

Indeed, in the sense that rap/poetry is work that is fundamentally oppositional to a dominant mainstream aesthetic, the idea of such a traditional method of poetic composition as accentual/syllabic metrical construction seems antithetical. Why would young, mostly undereducated, marginalized rap/poets, trying to be "true" to hip hop, adopt a style of poetic construction that mimics Milton, Keats, or Shelley? The short answer is they wouldn't. And they don't. It is a purely artificial and largely unproductive exercise to scan rap/poems. (In moments of rare idleness, though, I might do it anyway.)

The fact is, every line of a rap/poem *can* be scanned to reveal its structure. But when all of the lines of a rap/poem are scanned and then compared to each other, it is rare that a solid form emerges. Rap/poets do indeed move effortlessly from pentameter to hexameter to tetrameter and so forth, but they do so not in service to some external desire to achieve a traditional poetic form. They do so in service to the rhyme itself. This, then, becomes my preferred way of talking about rap/poetic structure. Even though I've spent some time talking about the scanning process, I do not recommend it. Instead, I encourage the readers/listeners who want to investigate the construction of rap/poems to focus more on the rhyme pattern as opposed to the metrical and syllabic computations we use in scansion.

When the system of rhyme is used to establish structure, we can dispense with issues that focus completely on line composition. In the context of hip hop culture, this makes perfect sense. If poetry is at the heart of the hip hop beat, rhyme is at the core of the poetry.

Rhyme has many beneficial qualities, but one of its main attributes is its ability to function in a cultural context. Rhyme can convey information, history, and story in a digestible way—in a way that is like slipping into a family member's coat. The smell of it, the feel of it is oddly familiar. Natural. And rhyme is easily remembered. Rhyme has functioned this way since the beginning of speech. The Africans, Egyptians, Greeks, Chinese, and all other great cultures used rhyme as the conduit for expressing humor, satire, love, and conflict.

So, instead of focusing our attention on the lines of the rap/poem, we have instead decided to privilege the rhyme over the line. That is, line length, line breaks, and all things metrical about the poem we accept as *influencing* the structure of a rap/poem, but it cannot *define* that poem's structure. What does define structure is the rhyme scheme. How the poem moves along its own story line, how quickly the rhyme is executed, and how soon after a pattern develops is that pattern modified or changed altogether: these are the areas we choose to focus on rather than its measured construction. In short, we have come to consider and evaluate rap/poets by their deft manipulation of rhyme. While rap/poets may not be thinking about iambs or anapests in a traditional sense, they are most definitely thinking about rhyme and its construction.

There are three types of rap/poets. *Functional* rap/poets who use a basic rap/poetic structure. *Smooth* rap/poets who use a modified basic structure. And *virtuoso* rap/poets who use complex weaves of basic and modified techniques as well as rhyme variations to perfection. The basic structure might best be found in one of the first commercially successful rap/poems, "The Breaks," by Kurtis Blow. Incidentally, when we look at rhyme, we don't use scansion but a simple notation of each rhyming word.

Brakes on a bus, brakes on a car	A
Breaks to make you a superstar	A
Breaks to win and breaks to lose	B
But these here breaks will rock your shoes	B

These four lines typify the basic rap/poetry structure. By basic, we mean the rhyme occurs in a series of two-line couplets, each line terminating in an "end-stop," that is, with each line completing a thought. There is nothing mysterious or fancy happening in these lines, but they function marvelously as a mechanism of communication.

Indeed, it is the basic form of rap/poetry that assures McDonald's, General Mills, or Pepsi-Cola that it can be easily appropriated for their commercial uses. It is also the basic form of rap/poetry that allows for so much inferior work. If the value of rap/poetry were to be found completely in this form, it would be largely valueless. Still, when this form is extended, it can become almost breathless, as happens when we catch up with Kurtis Blow's "The Breaks" in the next stanza:

If your woman steps out with another man	A
And she runs off with him to Japan	A
And the IRS says they want to chat	B
And you can't explain why you claimed your cat	B
And Ma Bell sends you a whopping bill	C
With eighteen phone calls to Brazil	C
And you borrowed money from the mob	D
And yesterday you lost your job	D
Well, these are the breaks	OFF

In a basic rhyme structure like this, the poet is locked into a scheme that is so predictable, only a novel story line or surprising word choice will satisfy us. Fortunately, "The Breaks" is such a poem. Its humor and cleverness are the driving energy. In the early days of rap, this form was the most convenient, the most portable and easiest to learn. But as the art form evolved, poets became dissatisfied with the limitations of the basic structure and began to modify it, to complicate it with more intense and immediate images, language, and meanings.

The modified basic structure can be demonstrated by All Natural's "50 Years":

1. Now everybody	OFF
2. fast forward to the future, the year, 2-0-4-4	A
3. And let me tell what's in store	A
4. Just so you won't be surprised [B] when we blow up, before your eyes	B
5. And when you watch my kids grow up, then, you'll realize	B
6. that my literary talent was genetic	C
7. Copasetic [C] not pathetic [C], but poetic[C]ally prophetic	C
8. Now 50 years down the line, we gon' all look back	D
9. and say that hip-hop, in 1995 was wack	D

The smooth structure can be easily distinguished from the basic in a number of ways. First, the smooth structure makes use of the off rhyme, usually as a way to drive a point home. Second, it modifies the basic by addition: it adds one or more rhymes to the basic couplet form, creating rhyming sets of three or more. Third, partly driven by the use of additional rhymes within a set, the smooth form makes use of internal rhymes. These internal rhymes, such as those in lines 6 and 7, add energy to the poem and completely upset the predictability of the basic structure. The smooth rap/poets are aware of the general ineffectiveness of the basic structure over a long complicated poem. They are much more conscious of the need to "rupture" the predictability of the basic.

An example of the virtuoso structure can be found in Common's "Between Me, You, & Liberation."

1. She rested her head upon my chest	A
2. Sensed liberation in between breaths	A
3. Wonder if sex [A] is what she found it in	B
4. Peace, found* it laying down with men	B
5. Wasn't there to judge her [C], many ways I loved her	C
6. It was more than bodies we shared with each other	C
7. We laid under the cover of friends	OFF
8. A place where many lovers began	D
9. I began [D], to feel her body shake in my hand	D
10. Body* language, it's so hard trying to understand	D
11. Usually after sex, it's a good feel	E
12. Took by silence, emotion stood still	E
13. I could feel [E], her tears spill [E], from her grill	E
14. Hurt from before that began to build	E (close)
15. She told me* hold me*, a story*, she assembled it	F
16. Tellin' it [F], trying not to remember it	F
17. It [F] was a story of innocence taken	G
18. Thought she could redeem, through love makin'	G
19. When she was eight* she was raped* by her father	H
20. And tried to escape* through multiple sex partners	H (close)
21. Felt pitiful, she had only learned,	I
22. To love through the physical, inside it burned	I
23. My heart turned [I], I thought of what this man did	J
24. She forgave him, she grew to understand it	OFF
25. Her soul was tired and never really rested	K
26. Only with men through aggression	K (close)
27. Said it was a blessing and it happened for a reason	L
28. By speaking it, she found freedom	L (close)
29. Between me and you	OFF

In this poem, the first six lines appear to be basic, but the use of internal rhymes changes that. The word "sex" in line 3 is dropped to rhyme with "breath" in line 2, thus extending the "A" rhyme set beyond the couplet of the basic rap structure. Common also uses repetition of specific words (marked by an asterisk) such as "found" in line 4 and "body" in line 10 in succeeding lines that don't function as rhymes as much as echoes of the previous line. I particularly like Common's use of the off rhyme, especially in line 24. This, I believe, forces the reader/listener to stop and contemplate meaning. It is the turning point in this poem, with the main point coming in line 28.

Common is also constantly changing the rhyme formation. This technique is common among virtuoso rap/poets. Nothing prepares us for the bursting, propulsive energy of lines 11 thru 14 where he rhymes six times in the "E" rhyme set. Virtuoso rap/poets will also make creative use of "close" rhymes—words that, when sounded out in a particular context, mimic rhyme, as in "rested" at the end of line 25 and "aggression" in line 26. In fact, it is the "est" of "rested" that rhymes with the "gres" of "aggression. In the end, the challenge of the rap/poet, as it pertains to structure, is to establish a rhyme pattern that is organic, that is as complex as it needs to be to carry the message of the poem, and that has an inherent flow.

FLOW

Flow is created from the effectiveness of the structure. Structure alone does not establish quality. But when flow is achieved, it is because the structure is present and establishes the environment in which the poet can flow. In other words, all of the images, rhymes, and ideas held within the body of a rap/poem must coalesce into a whole. And the whole must move fluidly from beginning to end. This fluid movement—sometimes breakneck, sometimes languid—we call the flow. There are times when a rap/poet is deep within the rhyme pattern. The poem is alive with energy, and we know that "the poet's flowin'." In the final analysis, when we measure the effectiveness of a rap/poem's structure, we are judging its flow as well. In Rob Base and DJ E-Z Rock's "Times Are Gettin' Ill," the flow is perfectly constructed:

> Just last week I had a good thing goin
> The money was flowin
> I had a notion, I made a motion
> To get a girl with love and devotion
> I went to a disco . . . ordered a bottle of Cisco
> Took a seat, and I looked around
> Bobbin' my head to the sound
> Of the D.J., OK, this is what I'm tryin' ta say
> I heard a scream (AAAAAAH!)
> Then a shot rang out (BOOOOOM . . . BOOOOOM)
> That's when I got the hell out

We can articulate why the flow works so well. Embedded in this rap/poem, as the story unfolds, is a rising energy that comes from the basic rhyme structure and that keeps our focus on the actions happening in the poem. In fact, when the basic rhyme structure is effectively employed, we almost never pay attention to it. The predictability of the basic, when married to an interesting story, keeps our attention on the story.

One of my favorite rap/poems is Pete Rock and CL Smooth's "They Reminisce Over You," another poem that uses the basic structure to good effect. Here is the second stanza:

> When I date back I recall a man off the family tree
> My right hand Poppa Doc I see
> Took me from a boy to a man so I always had a father
> When my biological didn't bother
> Taking care of this so who am I to bicker
> Not a bad ticker but I'm clocking pop's liver
> But you can never say that his life is through
> 5 kids at 21 believe he got a right to
> Here we go while I check the scene
> With the Portuguese lover at the age of 14
> The same age, front page, no fuss
> But I bet you all your dough, they live longer than us
> Never been senile, that's where you're wrong
> But give the man a taste and he's gone
> Noddin off, to sleep to a jazz tune
> I can hear his head banging on the wall in the next room
> I get the pillow and hope I don't wake him
> For this man do cuss, hear it all in verbatim
> Telling me how to raise my boy unless he's taking over
> I said pop maybe when you're older
> We laughed all night about the hookers at the party
> My old man standing yelling "good God, almighty"
> Use your condom, take sips of the brew
> When they reminisce over you, for real

This rap/poem is constructed in the basic form, but the story is powerful. The inventive language conjures a memory that transcends that of one person. This is a memory that we all can share in. Our lives may be different from the poets', but we can substitute events and situations that happened to us for those of the poets, and the truth of the poem survives. Their reminiscences trigger our own. All of this keeps us moving from rhyme to rhyme in the sweetest flow.

By contrast, Jean Grae, in "Keep Living," employs the virtuoso to capture her flow:

1. grew up child of an alcoholic sister too schizophrenic
2. Already inherited one and both are genetic
3. when the sun falls, I get no sleep
4. nights are filled with party and bullshit, bacardi and full clips
5. just to deal with it
6. got a full heart but I don't feel with it no more
7. I have the fury of the women scorned
8. Just live my life like the x-files and trust nobody
9. Forgetting everyone
10. Now I am just for getting the money
11. Funny how shit can change and switch up
12. Fragile to rip on you
13. I spent too much of my young life just trying to stick shit up
14. I am living day by day now every step is play by play
15. hand to mouth just trying to make these moments count

In this poem, Grae demonstrates the way in which rupture amplifies the effectiveness of the rhyme. Rupture is the opposite of flow, and when a flow is consciously ruptured, the returning flow is made more intense. Rap/poets purposefully rupture flow to underscore a particular point. Rupture is usually caused by an off rhyme: "when the sun falls, I get no sleep" (line 3) does not rhyme with line 4 or line 2, and it disrupts the flow of the basic Grae had going in the first rhyme set. We are forced to pause, to consider the impact of the sadness evinced in the first two lines. The complexity, the gravitas of this rap/poem requires a form that allows us access to its entire dimension. The virtuoso form does that and provides a flow that equals the depth of the poem.

* * *

Taken together, these elements can frame an in-depth discussion about any rap/poem. This is perhaps the most important function of the system of analysis and review of rap/poetry offered above. I have, of course, used it to literally measure the strengths of a given rap/poem in comparison with another. This system can be used that way, as a way of ranking them. My students have had great debate and discussion in the process of doing just that. But its real value, I believe, rests in the journey. For example, when a group of people who associate with each other are all familiar with a specific rap/poem, the conversation that is possible, talking about meaning, texture, saturation, and so forth, yields all manner of opinion. Besides, it forces us to value the expression as art. Rap/poetry.

NOTES

1. Stephen Henderson, *Understanding the New Black Poetry* (Morrow, 1973).

2. Frantz Fanon, *Black Skin, White Masks*, trans. Charles Lam Markmann (Grove, 1967), 17.

3. Tricia Rose, *Black Noise* (Wesleyan, 1994).

4. Russell Potter, *Spectacular Vernaculars* (SUNY Press, 1995); Henry Louis Gates Jr., *The Signifying Monkey: A Theory of African-American Literary Criticism* (Oxford University Press, 1989).

5. Gwendolyn D. Pough, *Check It While I Wreck It* (Northeastern, 2004), 19.

6. Pough, *Check It While I Wreck It*, 93.

7. Thulani Davis, "The Height of Disrespect," *Village Voice*, March 9, 2004.

8. In *Check It While I Wreck It*, Gwendolyn Pough provides a thorough discussion of the history and significance of women in rap/poetry.

9. Rose, *Black Noise*.

8

The Aesthetics: A Summary

Rap/poetry is and, from all appearances, will continue to be a significant contribution to African American literature. It is a contribution that goes largely unacknowledged, however, because so much attention is focused on the inferior, shallow, simpleminded, and inefficacious rap/poems. It is true, sadly, that a great deal of rap/poetry is caught in a loop, engaged in display and discussion of the basest and lowest standards of life. Ethics, morality, and spirituality are often expressed in terms of acquisition and material gain. Opportunism and accumulation are commonly found in the meanings of some rap/poetry.

Although this art form does have these problems, it still remains the most vibrant element in the landscape of African American literature. This is due in some degree to the sheer quantity of rap/poetry that is produced. It is easy to paint this work with too broad a brush. The good and exemplary get lost in the flurry of profanity, party rhymes, and braggadocio.

But it is also true that there has been no other time in the history of black people in America when they have had access to the technology of artistic production, the technology of distribution, and the willingness to display their unheralded literary capacity. What is remarkable, however, is that this literary capacity erupted in spite of and in defiance of a system of education that does not effectively do its job.

The elitism of American literary culture, with its agents, editors, and publishers, clearly marginalizes voices that are not from the mainstream. American literary critics, reviewers, agents, and editors, to an alarming degree, know very little about African American literary traditions. Consequently, they do not privilege those traditions and have no interest in their maintenance. I suppose this, too, is largely due to the educational system.

But young developing poets can now bypass that system. And, in so doing, they also escape rigorous reading. In the preceding pages, we have tried to begin a discussion about such a reading. We advocate seeing through the music and the beat of rap—moving beyond the trappings of both true and bogus expressions of hip hop culture—to find the poetry that is there. Once we locate the poetry in rap, we are able to validate it as the sustenance and cultural continuity that poetry provides. In other words, rap/poetry articulates the world that stares back at the rap/poet.

Now that we are left with only the words, we have attempted to outline a way of reading rap/poetry that yields both its contemporary and historical literary value. This way of reading may or may not correspond to any standing literary critical theory, but it does identify a way of reading rap/poetry that encourages the reader to step beyond the dominance of the beat and to see rap/poetry's many dimensions. It is an approach to rap/poetry that allows the reader to make judgments about its construction, its durability, and perhaps even its value. And it is an approach that is based on the components within rap. We have not superimposed a system of critical review but rather looked at rap from the inside out to define its elements.

I believe that nearly every conversation about rap is incomplete and probably specious if rap's literary elements have not been fully considered. To simply bemoan the abstract social implications of rap—to charge it with damaging the black community, for example—without doing the basic tasks of critical reading and comparing and contrasting rap/poems renders all opinions thin. There are too many discussions about rap in which neither proponent or opponent can quote extensively from a variety of rap/poems.

As our capacity to perform these kinds of analytical activities with rap/poetry increases, our conversations about it will become more accurate and more sophisticated. This has been the primary motivating energy for writing this book.

And as we get better about talking about rap—acquiring the ability to distinguish those rap/poems that are outstanding examples of literary and cultural achievement from those that are bad imitations or worse—we will discover that rap/poets (African American, African, white, Asian, Latino, Native American, and all other races and nationalities) have benefited from the literary history and progression of African American literature. We will discover the wide and dynamic range of topics with which these poets engage. We will marvel at the complex and textured images they portray of the people around them and of the life and struggle that encapsulates urban areas. And we will be amazed at the capacity these young poets have to propel us to new understandings about ourselves through their mastery of the parts of speech and their facility with words.

In essence, the heart of the beat—the poetry of rap—provides us with a continuous loop of information and images of ourselves. If you are offended by it, in a way, you should be. The language rap/poets use is the language we use. The images they craft are no different from the ones crafted by screen-writers and crime scene reporters. If their ethics, morals, and values are troubling, it is because of what we have shown them of ourselves. Indeed, we are them.

Outro: The Professor Revisited

Not long ago, I went to Gary, Indiana, to give a speech. My host, an African American woman who was the leader of the organization that had extended the invitation, met me at the airport. When I opened the door to her car, a compact disc fell out and clattered to the ground. I picked it up, instinctively looking to see who the artist was, but there was no label on it. I held it up to her as I closed the car door and settled into my seat. She took it from me and looked quizzically at it.

"Was this in the car?" she asked. I nodded. "Hmm, well it isn't mine. I bet it's my son's." She proceeded to tell me a little about her son, who was fourteen. She said that recently he'd started getting into trouble and that his grades had suddenly started to slip. It made me curious about him. Something about the developing identities in young African American men consistently intrigues me. There is so much sweetness there. So much potential. You can see it, feel it, and almost touch it as it begs for nourishment. And this need too often goes unmet. Here, in the world of the black adolescent, one can engage in the most intense discussions about hope, love, and sadness. Even though I was the visitor, a stranger to this woman and her son (whom I hadn't even met yet), I was instantly intrigued and wanted to know her and her son better.

When I asked if she knew what was on the disc, she said, "No." So, again, on instinct, I suggested we play it. She slipped it into the CD player and in a flash, the top single of the moment, 50 Cent's megahit "In Da Club," filled the car. Her eyes widened as she turned to me. I knew immediately that she was surprised. "I told that boy I didn't want him listening to that stuff." She quickly searched through her purse, pulled out her cell phone, and called her son.

"What's this music you have on this CD?" she asked him. After she got off the phone, she told me he "claimed" it wasn't his but his friend's. She told me a little about his friend, someone I think she felt was leading her son astray. I sensed she believed that the CD was her son's and that he was trying to defy her ban on rap music.

Later that night, after I gave my speech, two teenaged boys appeared before me. I knew immediately who they were. "So you teach a class on rap, like how to be a rapper?" one of them asked me. I told him no, I taught a class on how to listen to rap, how to make choices and choose the rap/poetry that fits you, that reflects who you are. I then asked him what kind of rap he liked, besides 50. He smiled at me and pointed to his friend, telling me that he was intent on keeping up the lie that the disc wasn't his. I asked them to walk me outside to get some air.

The sky was dark, but you could feel rain coming over the horizon. There is nothing like the midwestern sky under threat of rain or the full spray of sunlight; either one can ignite the imagination. The two boys commenced listing their favorites for me. Most of their favorites were CDs that I probably would not listen to. But they were interested in different things than I was. They didn't care much about positive images of black men, empowering messages from and about women, rap/poems that promoted humanistic or spiritual growth. They were interested more in the edginess of the hardcore, the party, and the aimless bluster of the thug that occupies the popular airwaves.

But in fifteen minutes or so, I could tell that it truly was his friend who called the shots. He was the one who wanted to be a rapper. He was the one who articulated the need to "keep it real from the streets." You can't change the minds of teenaged boys in thirty minutes, and I didn't really try. I only reiterated the importance of actually thinking about what you listen to—to think about it as if it actually represents who you are and not the other way around.

The next morning when his mother picked me up for the long drive back to the Chicago airport, I told her that I'd met and talked with her son and his friend. She was, of course, quite curious about what I thought. By this time, I was under the influence of a malady that affects those of us who arrive at a new destination, address a group by giving a reading or lecture, have dinner with people you might not ever see again, and leave by air the following morning: you feel like you know them. In the matter of an hour, you can care about them and their families, about the problems they have with their bosses, and so forth. It's quite profound really. At any rate, I simply said, meaning every word, "You need to spend more time with your son. He needs your help."

And the Professor needed ours. His poetry flew over our heads like cigarette smoke. We heard these words with which we were only vaguely familiar, combined with words we had no capacity to understand and formed into statements that left us scratching our heads and laughing at him. At *him*.

When all the time, he was the one giving gifts. Expression is the gift. We may not know what to do with that gift. We may actually misunderstand its meaning and purpose, condemning or ridiculing it. But it is really a gift. It is up to us to comprehend its significance before we dismiss it. I am comfortable with dismissing some of it, but only after I have made the honest effort to identify the reason for its existence and its effectiveness in achieving that purpose.

At the end of my course, I ask my students to answer two questions: "What is the function of rap/poetry?" and "What is common to all rap/poems?" My answers to those questions are quite straightforward. The function of rap/poetry is to structure the world in a way that puts the poet at its center. And what is common is the desire—the need—to speak and to express oneself. All rap/poetry does that. But only some of it works for me. Only some of it speaks words I can hear. Only some of it rings true.

There is no element in the conventional discussion of poetry, in its classic sense, that is not employed consciously or unconsciously by rap/poets. The best rap/poets, in their natural voices, do find the truth of their lives in these poems. And, like good poets, they are often unpredictable. Which brings us full circle. Back to the lights illuminated by Countee Cullen, Margaret Walker, Sterling Brown, Zora Neale Hurston, Jean Toomer, Sonia Sanchez, Langston Hughes, and many others. They chose to convert and subvert the English language to do their bidding. And rap/poets stand in their shadows.

Poetry is the most natural, truest statement we can make about a feeling, a thing, or a person. And rap/poets are steadily pumping the words directly into our ears, as if responding to the weight of Baraka's call in the concluding stanza of "Black Art":

> We want a black poem. And a
> Black World.
> Let the world be a Black Poem
> And Let All Black People Speak This Poem
> Silently
> Or LOUD.

Appendix: The Thematic Categories of Rap/Poetry

Over a period of ten years, we have attempted to group the corpus of rap/poetry by theme as a way of managing the enormous quantity of rap that is produced. In each category there are effective and interesting poems. In each category there are feeble, even miserable examples of wasted time. But what is brilliant is marvelously so—and important—and it should not be banished or denigrated on the vapor of its failed companions.

Perhaps even more important, in each category there exists an "underground" element. The underground is where new rhyming techniques come into being. It is also where rap/poets who have not yet become popular are free to experiment with meaning, language, and imagery. The underground is considered the locus of the purest expression of hip hop—the sound of hip hop before it can be commoditized, commercialized, and exploited. It is the source of rap/poetry's capacity to change and grow. It is at the basement level where hip hop gets its vital energy.

When poets rise up out of the basement of rap, they step into an industry. Most of them are changed forever. What was once lifeblood sometimes becomes paycheck. But some poets maintain a desire for clarity and dynamism through it all. Rap/poets like Eminem, Mos Def, the Black Eyed Peas, Little Brother, De La Soul, Slug, Brother Ali, Aceyalone, among many others, were once considered underground rappers.

By dividing the rap/poems into categories, we can see immediately the diversity of this poetry and not succumb to the instinctive urge some people have to group all rap/poetry into one stinking pile of noise. What follows is a brief description of the categorical labels and some examples of rap/poems in each category. The works listed here do not necessarily represent the best. Of course, it is not possible to include all of the rap/poems that merit discussion and admiration, but one of the goals of this work is to demonstrate the diversity of rap/poetry.

IN THE TRADITION

This category includes the formative and proto-rap/poetic expressions. It includes rap/poems in the tradition of early rap, such as rap battles, party rhymes, and the dozens. Traditional rap/poems often express the pure competitive aspects of the art form. Perhaps because the earliest rap/poetry, after the party rhymes, were attempts at self-promotion and self-identification, and were clear efforts to elevate one's profile by denigrating someone else, this category includes those classic verbal (mostly) battles between rap/poets.

Selected Rap/Poems in the Tradition

"Planet Rock" by Afrika Bambaataa
"How You Like Me Now" by Kool Moe Dee on *How Ya Like Me Now*
"Roxanne's Revenge" by Roxanne Shante on *Roxanne's Revenge 12"*
"Times Are Gettin' Ill" by Rob Base and DJ E-Z Rock on *It Takes Two*
"Kill That Noise" by MC Shan on *Down by Law*
"Paid in Full" by Eric B. and Rakim on *Paid in Full*
"Ether" by Nas on *Stillmatic*
"Final Hour" by Lauryn Hill on *The Miseducation of Lauryn Hill*
"Right Here" by Pharoahe Monch on *Internal Affairs*
"Takeover" by Jay Z on *The Blueprint*
"My Philosophy" by BDP on *By All Means Necessary*
"I Know You Got Soul" by Eric B. and Rakim on *Paid in Full*
"Let's Get It Started" by MC Hammer on *Let's Get It Started*
"Don't Cry Big Girls" by MC Lyte on *Lyte as a Rock*

CRIME AND PUNISHMENT

The crime and punishment category includes rap/poems about crime and the response to those crimes as well as poems written from the perspective of a criminal or rap/poems that have a main focus on the description of criminal actions or lifestyle.

Selected Rap/Poems on Crime and Punishment

"A Bird in the Hand" by Ice Cube on *Death Certificate*
"D'Evils" by Jay Z on *Reasonable Doubt*

"C.R.E.A.M." by Wu-Tang Clan on *Enter the Wu-Tang (36 Chambers)*
"Dance with the Devil" by Immortal Technique on *Revolutionary Vol. 1*
"Gimme the Loot" by Notorious B.I.G. on *Ready to Die*
"Walk Like a Man" by Murs on *Murs 3:16: The 9th Edition*
"Slippin" by Lil Kim on *The Naked Truth*

SOCIAL CRITIQUE

Issues of race, culture, history, education, politics, and more have been combined into this category. So the variety of poetry in this category spans a wide swath of interests and concerns.

Selected Rap/Poems of Social Critique

"A Song for Assata" by Common on *Like Water for Chocolate*
"White America" by Eminem on *The Eminem Show*
"Satisfied?" by J-Live on *All of the Above*
"A Million Eyes" by Apani B on *A Million Eyes 12" Single*
"Alive on Arrival" by Ice Cube on *Death Certificate*
"Love's Gonna Getcha" by BDP on *Edutainment*
"White Man'z World" by Tupac on *The Don Killuminati: The 7 Day Theory*
"Beautiful Things" by Bahamadia on *BB Queen*
"Who Protects Us from You?" by BDP on *Ghetto Music: The Blueprint*
"Beef' by BDP on *Edutainment*
"Word to the Mother (Land)" by Big Daddy Kane on *Long Live the Kane*
"Hypocrisy is the Greatest Luxury" by Disposable Heroes of Hiphoprisy on *Hypocrisy Is the Greatest Luxury*
"Peace Is Not the Word to Play" by Main Source on *Breaking Atoms*
"Block Party" by Jean Grae on *Attack of the Attacking Things*
"Cleopatra" by Yo Yo on *Black Pearl*
"Conflict Diamonds" by Lupe Fiasco on *Lupe Fiasco Touch the Sky (Mixtape) DJ Enyce*
"Georgia Bush" by Lil Wayne on *Lil Wayne DJ Drama Dedication 2 (Mixtape) Gangsta Grillz*
"By the Time I Get to Arizona" by Public Enemy on *Apocalypse 91 . . . The Enemy Strikes Back*

INNER-CITY LIFE

The inner-city or streetlife category includes poems about life in the inner city, poverty, the urban struggle, and dealing with life on the street.

Selected Rap/Poems of Inner-City Life

"Cappuchino" by MC Lyte on *Eyes on This*
"For Women" by Talib Kweli on *Reflection Eternal: Train of Thought*
"I Seen a Man Die" by Scarface on *I Seen a Man Die 12"*
"The March" by Aceyalone on *A Book of Human Language*
"The Message" by Melle Mel on *The Message 12"*
"The Ghetto" by Too $hort on *Short Dog's in the Big House*
"Mind Playin Tricks on Me" by Scarface on *The Diary*

GENDER DISCOURSE

This category includes issues of gender agency, power, oppression, and sexuality/gender. Poems deal with issues of sexuality, misogyny, and misandry.

Selected Rap/Poems of Gender Discourse

"God's Gift" by Jean Grae on *Attack of the Attacking Things*
"Shitty Situation" by Conscious Daughters on *Ear to the Street*
"Wonder Why They Call U Bytch" by Tupac on *All Eyez on Me*
"My Bitches" by Eve on *Let There Be Eve: Ruff Ryders First Lady . . .*
"U.N.I.T.Y." by Queen Latifah on *Black Reign*
"Doo Wop (That Thing)" by Lauryn Hill on *The Miseducation of Lauryn Hill*

RELATIONSHIPS

These are poems of love and other relationships.

Selected Rap/Poems on Relationships

"You Got Me" by the Roots on *Things Fall Apart*
"You're All I Need (Remix)" by Method Man on *You're All I Need (Remix) 12"*
"Between Me, You, & Liberation" by Common on *Electric Circus*
"I Need Love" by LL Cool J on *Bigger and Deffer*
"The Light" by Common on *Like Water for Chocolate*
"Love Song" by Jean Grae on *Attack of the Attacking Things*
"Paper Thin" by MC Lyte on *Lyte as a Rock*
"I Confess" by Bahamadia on *Kollage*

ROOTS

The roots category encompasses neighborhood, family, and friends. Poems are about growing up, family, neighborhood, and home.

Selected Rap/Poems of Roots

"Dance" by Nas on *God's Son*
"Dear Mama" by Tupac on *Me Against the World*
"They Reminisce Over You (T.R.O.Y.)" by Pete Rock and CL Smooth on *Mecca and the Soul Brother*
"Juicy" by Notorious B.I.G. on *Ready to Die*
"Friends" by Whodini on *Escape*
"Black Girl Pain" by Talib Kweli on *The Beautiful Struggle*

ON HIP HOP

This category includes poems concerning hip hop itself.

Selected Rap/Poems on Hip Hop

"Moment of Clarity" by Jay Z on *The Black Album*
"Used to Love H.E.R." by Common on *Resurrection*
"Rape Over" by Mos Def on *The New Danger*
"Like Toy Soldiers" by Eminem on *Encore*
"The Listening" by Little Brother on *The Listening*
"Rap Game" by MC Lyte on *Bad As I Wanna Be*

LANGUAGE, SATIRE, AND PARODY

This category focuses on word play and where word play is the meaning of the poem.

Selected Rap/Poems on Language, Satire, and Parody

"They Want EFX" by Das EFX on *Dead Serious*
"Verses from the Abstract" by Q-Tip of A Tribe Called Quest on *The Low End Theory*
"Me Myself and I" by De La Soul on *3 Feet High and Rising*
"My Pen and My Pad" by Blackalicious on *The Craft*
"I Am I Be" by De La Soul on *Buhloone Mindstate*

"How to Rob" by 50 Cent on *Power of the Dollar*
"Can't Truss It" by Public Enemy on *Apocalypse 91 . . . The Enemy Strikes Back*
"Ebonics" by Big L on *The Big Picture*
"Niggaz 4 Life" by NWA on *Efil4zaggin*
"Prophets of Rage" by Public Enemy on *It Takes a Nation of Millions to Hold Us Back*
"3 the Hard Way" by Bahamadia on *Kollage*
"Fox That Rox the Box" by Antoinette on *Burnin' at 20 Below*

SPIRITUALITY

This category includes poems discussing any type of religious or spiritual feeling.

Selected Rap/Poems on Spirituality

"Take Me" by Jean Grae on *Bootleg of the Bootleg EP*
"Jesus Walks" by Kanye West on *College Dropout*
"Holy Smokes" by Aesop Rock on *Fast Cars, Danger, Fire and Knives*
"Fishin' 4 Religion" by Arrested Development on *3 Years, 5 Months & 2 Days in the Life of . . .*
"Ready to Meet Him" by DMX on *Flesh of My Flesh, Blood of My Blood*
"Interview with a Vampire" by Ras Kass on *Rasassination*
"Impossible" by Wu-Tang Clan on *Wu-Tang Forever*

About the Author

Alexs Pate is the author of five novels, including *Amistad* commissioned by Steven Spielberg's Dreamworks/SKG and based on the screenplay by David Franzoni, which became a *New York Times* best seller. The Black Caucus of the American Library Association selected his novel *West of Rehoboth* as the Honor Fiction Book in 2002. In February 2002, noted National Book Award novelist Charles Johnson chose Pate as an "Achiever Who Will Lead the Next Generation" in the area of literature. The list of eight "achievers" was published in *USA Today Weekend* along with a dialog between Johnson and Pate.

Pate recently completed the nonfiction work *The Past Is Perfect: Memoir of a Father/Son Reunion*. An excerpt appeared in *Black Renaissance Noire* (Fall 2007). He is currently at work on a new novel about a black pirate captain.

Pate's short stories and essays have appeared in *African American Literary Criticism: 1773–2000, Brotherman, Gumbo, After Hours, Dream Me Home Safely*, and other publications. His short story "Merry Christmas, Tamyra" was commissioned by National Public Radio's All Things Considered and was read on Christmas day 2002; Pate does periodic commentary for that same program. He was also one of three final judges for the 2003 PEN/ Faulkner Fiction Award.

His novel *Multicultiboho Sideshow* was awarded the 2000 Minnesota Book Award for the Novel. An excerpt from this satire on race, money, and innocence appeared in the November issue of *Code*. His novel *Finding Makeba* tells the story of a father and daughter who overcome the struggles of a disintegrating family to find each other; now in paperback, it was named by *Essence* magazine as one of the "top five family classics" and a book that every black woman should have on her bookshelf.

Pate's debut novel, *Losing Absalom*, was chosen as Best First Novel by the Black Caucus of the American Library Association and received a 1995 Minnesota Book Award for best fiction. An excerpt appears in the major anthology *Brotherman*. His first book of poetry, *Innocent*, was published in 1999. Pate also contributed the essay "Contemporary African American Literature: Anywhere the Wind Blows" to the anthology *Atlas of Literature* (1996), edited by Malcolm Bradbury.

His collaborative performance with Asian American poet David Mura was presented in the Walker Art Center's "Out There" series in January 1994 and again at the Painted Bride Arts Center in Philadelphia. He and David Mura have also co-written and starred in a short feature film, *Slowly This*, directed by Arthur Jafa, which aired nationally on PBS and is in current circulation at film festivals. In 1994, his play *Multicultiboho Sideshow* was performed at the Pillsbury House Theater under the direction of Ralph Remington. His essays and commentary have appeared in the *Utne Reader*, *Washington Post*, *Minneapolis Star and Tribune*, and *USA Today Weekend* among others. His fiction and poetry have appeared in numerous publications including *The Butterfly Tree*, *Indigene*, *Artpaper*, and *The North Stone Review*.

Pate is an assistant professor of Afro-American and African Studies at the University of Minnesota, where he teaches courses in writing and black literature, including "The Poetry of Rap." He has also served as a consultant on multicultural issues to the textbook publisher McDougal Littel.